Doug Li v. John Ross and Ross Construction Co., Inc.

Defendants' Materials

Third Edition

Paul J. Zwier

Professor of Law
Emory University School of Law

DOUG LI V. JOHN ROSS AND ROSS CONSTRUCTION CO., INC.

Defendants' Materials

Third Edition

Paul J. Zwier

Professor of Law
Emory University School of Law

NATIONAL INSTITUTE FOR TRIAL ADVOCACY

Address inquiries to:
Reprint Permission
National Institute for Trial Advocacy
1685 38th Street, Suite 200
Boulder, CO 80301-2735
Phone: (800) 225-6482
Fax: (720) 890-7069
E-mail: permissions@nita.org

ISBN 978-1-60156-432-0
eISBN 978-1-63282-709-8
FBA 1432

Printed in the United States of America

Official co-publisher of NITA.
WKLegaledu.com/NITA

CONTENTS

INTRODUCTION

This is an interference with business relations/interference with contract case brought in the state of Nita by Doug Li, dba Li Builders, against John Ross, Ross Construction, Inc. Mr. Li claims that he had a contract or significant business relation with Ms. Michelle Greenwood and claims that Mr. Ross improperly interfered with his relationship with Ms. Greenwood by making a series of improper and false statements about the quality of his work.

As a result of these statements, Mr. Li claims that Ms. Greenwood broke off her relationship with him and instead gave the contract to Mr. Ross. Mr. Ross is Mr. Li's brother-in-law. Mr. Li is a child of Chinese immigrants who came to the United States before Mr. Li was born. Ms. Greenwood was developing the Little Sisters of the Poor Convent into luxury condominiums. The project was known as the Warsaw. The total cost of the project was to be in the range of 18 to 22 million dollars. Both parties agree that standard profit to a general contractor in such a project is 10 percent of the total cost of the project.

This case can be tried one of two ways. For a more lengthy and complex trial, all three causes of action can be tried simultaneously. Alternately, to try the case in the usual four-and-one-half- to five-and-one-half-hour time frame, the defamation cause of action can be dismissed on defendant's motion for summary judgment. The plaintiff can make his record on the defamation claim, but focus primarily on the interference with business relations/interference with contract cause of action.

The applicable law is contained in the jury instructions that are set forth at the end of the case file.

All years in these materials are stated in the following form:

YR-0: Indicates the actual year in which the case is being tried (the present year).

YR-1: Indicates the next preceding year (please use the actual year, 20—).

YR-2: Indicates the second preceding year (please use the actual year, 20—).

Electronic files for the exhibits are available for download here:

Website: http://bit.ly/1P20Jea
Password: Li3

Witness List

The witnesses listed below are available to be deposed, and they are affiliated with the designated parties. Witnesses may be prepared for deposition by the party with whom they are affiliated. When a witness is deposed, the deposition shall be noticed and taken by counsel for the opposing party.

Plaintiff:	Doug/Debra Li
	Mary Ross Li/Mark Ross
	Abigail/Abe Goldstein
Defendant:	John/Joan Ross
	Martha Ross/Arthur Swanson
	Dave/Darleen Peters
	Michelle/Michael Greenwood
	Bob/Bette Johnson

STIPULATIONS

1. Doug Li has indicated that he is not going to sue Michelle Greenwood and that he hopes to do business with her sometime in the future.

2. Assume that the calendar on page 7 is correct.

3. The architect's report is the sole property of the architect. Doug Li has no property interest in the architect's report.

4. The law for the case is contained in the Jury Instructions located at the end of this case file.

5. The Warsaw project has now been completed. Ross's final bill was for $25,000,000. Ross reduced his profit to $200,000, or approximately 1 percent, to bring Greenwood's total cost of the project to $25,000,000.00.

CALENDAR

January

Su	M	T	W	Th	F	Sa
			1	2	3	4
5	6	7	8	9	10	11
12	13	14	15	16	17	18
19	20	21	22	23	24	25
26	27	28	29	30	31	

February

Su	M	T	W	Th	F	Sa
						1
2	3	4	5	6	7	8
9	10	11	12	13	14	15
16	17	18	19	20	21	22
23	24	25	26	27	28	

March

Su	M	T	W	Th	F	Sa
						1
2	3	4	5	6	7	8
9	10	11	12	13	14	15
16	17	18	19	20	21	22
23	24	25	26	27	28	29
30	31					

April

Su	M	T	W	Th	F	Sa
		1	2	3	4	5
6	7	8	9	10	11	12
13	14	15	16	17	18	19
20	21	22	23	24	25	26
27	28	29	30			

May

Su	M	T	W	Th	F	Sa
				1	2	3
4	5	6	7	8	9	10
11	12	13	14	15	16	17
18	19	20	21	22	23	24
25	26	27	28	29	30	31

June

Su	M	T	W	Th	F	Sa
1	2	3	4	5	6	7
8	9	10	11	12	13	14
15	16	17	18	19	20	21
22	23	24	25	26	27	28
29	30					

July

Su	M	T	W	Th	F	Sa
		1	2	3	4	5
6	7	8	9	10	11	12
13	14	15	16	17	18	19
20	21	22	23	24	25	26
27	28	29	30	31		

August

Su	M	T	W	Th	F	Sa
					1	2
3	4	5	6	7	8	9
10	11	12	13	14	15	16
17	18	19	20	21	22	23
24	25	26	27	28	29	30
31						

September

Su	M	T	W	Th	F	Sa
	1	2	3	4	5	6
7	8	9	10	11	12	13
14	15	16	17	18	19	20
21	22	23	24	25	26	27
28	29	30				

October

Su	M	T	W	Th	F	Sa
			1	2	3	4
5	6	7	8	9	10	11
12	13	14	15	16	17	18
19	20	21	22	23	24	25
26	27	28	29	30	31	

November

Su	M	T	W	Th	F	Sa
						1
2	3	4	5	6	7	8
9	10	11	12	13	14	15
16	17	18	19	20	21	22
23	24	25	26	27	28	29
30	31					

December

Su	M	T	W	Th	F	Sa
	1	2	3	4	5	
6	7	8	9	10	11	12
13	14	15	16	17	18	19
20	21	22	23	24	25	26
27	28	29	30	31		

IN THE CIRCUIT COURT OF NITA CITY, NITA

Doug Li, dba Li Builders	)	
	)	
Plaintiff	)	
	)	
v.	)	**COMPLAINT**
	)	
John Ross and	)	
Ross Construction Co., Inc.	)	No. C-1234
	)	
Defendants	)	

The plaintiff states:

FIRST CLAIM FOR RELIEF—INTERFERENCE WITH CONTRACTUAL RELATION

1. Plaintiff is engaged in business as a general building contractor in and around Nita City, Nita, and has been so engaged at all times pertinent hereto.

2. Defendants are in the business of commercial building and at all times pertinent hereto were so engaged. Their place of business is located at 5411 Patterson Avenue, Nita City, Nita.

3. On or about July 11, YR-2, Ms. Michelle Greenwood contracted with the plaintiff to renovate the Little Sisters of the Poor Convent (now known as the Warsaw) into condominiums for the sum of $21,998,790.00.

4. On or about July 11, YR-2, the defendants jointly and severally intentionally, maliciously, and improperly interfered with the plaintiff's contract with Ms. Greenwood and caused Ms. Greenwood to break her contract with the plaintiff.

5. As a proximate result of the actions of the defendants John Ross and Ross Construction Co., Inc., and each of them, they became liable to the plaintiff, jointly and severally, for a sum equal to $5,999,890.00, representing $1,999,890.00 in lost profits from the loss of the contract and representing $4,000,000.00 in lost profits from future contracts with Ms. Greenwood.

SECOND CLAIM FOR RELIEF—INTERFERENCE WITH PROSPECTIVE ECONOMIC ADVANTAGE

6. Plaintiff incorporates by reference Paragraphs 1 and 2.

7. On June 25, YR-2, the plaintiff and Ms. Greenwood entered into negotiations to make renovations on Ms. Greenwood's Little Sisters of the Poor condominium project. The plaintiff was to work with Ms. Greenwood's architect and prepare and provide designs and plans to Ms. Greenwood for the renovation of her development property. The renovation was to commence on August 15, YR-2.

8. On or about July 11, YR-2, the defendants jointly and severally intentionally, recklessly, and improperly made false and malicious statements about the plaintiff's business and business abilities to Ms. Greenwood by stating erroneously that the plaintiff did not have the experience in renovating historical buildings that the defendants did; that the plaintiff's work was "sloppy"; that the plaintiff was ineffective in dealing with and managing subcontractors; and that the plaintiff routinely failed to complete jobs in a timely fashion.

9. As a proximate result of the aforementioned false, malicious, slanderous statements, the plaintiff was damaged in his prospective economic relation with Ms. Greenwood. As a proximate result of the actions of the defendants, John Ross and Ross Construction Co., Inc., and each of them, became liable to the plaintiff, jointly and severally, for a sum equal to $5,999,890.00.

THIRD CLAIM FOR RELIEF—SLANDER

10. Plaintiff incorporates by reference paragraphs 1 and 2.

11. That on or about July 11, YR-2, at the Nita Country Club in Nita City, the defendant, John Ross, in the presence and hearing of Ms. Michelle Greenwood and other persons unknown to the plaintiff, spoke false and defamatory words concerning the plaintiff, the substance of which was that Mr. Li was less experienced in historical renovations than the defendant, John Ross, and that Mr. Li was ineffective in dealing with his sub- contractors, sloppy in his work, and routinely failed to complete jobs in a timely fashion.

12. That the defendant's statement was not protected by a qualified privilege; or in the alternative, that if it was so protected, the defendant abused that privilege and lost his protection by making the statement with malice toward the plaintiff or with a reckless disregard for his interests.

13. That prior to the defendant's speaking the false and defamatory words concerning the plaintiff, the plaintiff had entered into or was about to enter into a contract to renovate Ms. Greenwood's property for $2,442,800.00; that as a result of the defendant's speaking such false and defamatory words, Ms. Greenwood refused to go forward in her relationship with the plaintiff.

14. That by reason of such slanderous publication, the plaintiff was denied the benefits of the contract and incurred a substantial loss of earning amounting to $5,999,890.00, representing $1,999,890.00 in lost profits from the loss of the contract, and representing $4,000,000.00 in lost profits from future contracts with Ms. Greenwood. In addition, the plaintiff was subjected to contempt and ridicule and was injured in his reputation and has suffered great pain and mental anguish, all to the plaintiff's damage.

FOURTH CLAIM FOR RELIEF—PUNITIVE DAMAGES

15. Plaintiff realleges paragraphs 1–15.

16. That Defendants made the statements with malice toward the plaintiff or with reckless disregard for the interests of the plaintiff.

17. That the defendants should be punished for such malicious statements.

18. That by reason of such malicious statements, the plaintiff demands judgment against the defendants for punitive damages in the amount of $20,000,000.00 and for such other relief the Court deems equitable and just.

WHEREFORE Plaintiff, Doug Li, demands judgment against the defendants, jointly and severally, in the sum of $5,999,890.00 under Counts One and Two; against defendant John Ross in the amount of $1,000,000.00 under Count Three; against the defendants jointly and severally for $20,000,000.00 in punitive damages, and for interest, costs, and for such other relief as the Court deems equitable and just.

Dated: August 25, YR-2

JURY DEMAND

Plaintiff demands a trial by jury in this action.

by:

Harold Baker
Attorney for Plaintiff
Suite 1200
UVB Bank Building
Nita City, Nita 23219

RETURN OF SUMMONS

I hereby certify that on August 27, YR-2, the above complaint and the summons were personally served on John Ross and Ross Construction Co., Inc. by serving John Ross at 5411 Patterson Ave., Nita City, Nita, 22321.

Frank Burns
Process Server

IN THE CIRCUIT COURT OF NITA CITY, NITA

Doug Li, dba Li Builders	)	
	)	
Plaintiff	)	
	)	
v.	)	
	)	**ANSWER**
John Ross and	)	
Ross Construction Co., Inc.	)	
	)	No. C-1234
Defendants	)	

JOINT ANSWER

John Ross, and Ross Construction Co., Inc., for their answer to the plaintiff's Complaint, state and allege as follows:

I

Deny each and every matter and thing, subject or allegation except as hereinafter admitted or answered by a qualified response.

II

Admit allegations set forth in paragraphs 1, 2.

III

Deny allegations set forth in paragraphs 3, 4, 5, 6, 8, 9, 10, 11, 12, 13, 14, 16, 17, and 18 of Plaintiff's Complaint.

IV

That as to allegations set forth in paragraph 7 of the plaintiff's Complaint, these answering defendants have insufficient information to form a belief as to the truth of those allegations.

AFFIRMATIVE DEFENSE

V

As to the claim for punitive damages, any amount awarded by a jury would violate defendants U.S. constitutional right to due process.

WHEREFORE, the defendants, John Ross, and Ross Construction Co., Inc., demand judgment of dismissal with prejudice of the plaintiff's complaint together with costs and disbursements herein incurred.

Dated: September 17, YR-2

Respectfully submitted,

Fred Smith

Fred Smith
Attorney for Defendant

IN THE CIRCUIT COURT OF NITA CITY, NITA

Doug Li, dba Li Builders)	
)	
Plaintiff)	**DEFENDANT'S MOTION FOR**
)	**SUMMARY JUDGMENT TO**
v.)	**PLAINTIFF'S SLANDER**
)	**CLAIM**
John Ross and)	
Ross Construction Co., Inc.)	NO. 1234
)	
Defendants)	

Comes now the defendant, John Ross, by counsel, and moves this Honorable court to strike Plaintiff's Claim for Relief for Slander on the grounds and for the reasons set forth in the accompanying Memorandum in Support of Motion for Summary Judgment.

Fred Smith

Fred Smith
Attorney for Defendant

Doug Li, dba Li Builders	)
	)
	) **MEMORANDUM IN SUPPORT OF**
Plaintiff	) **DEFENDANT'S MOTION FOR**
	) **SUMMARY JUDGMENT ON**
v.	) **PLAINTIFF'S SLANDER CLAIM**
	)
John Ross and	)
Ross Construction Inc.,	) NO. 1234
	)
Defendants	)

FACTS

On or about February 2, YR-1, the plaintiff served on the defendant a motion for judgment including a claim for relief for slander (a copy of the plaintiff's motion for judgment is attached).

Paragraph eleven (11) of same read that on or about July 11, YR-2, at the Nita Country Club, in the City of Nita, the defendant, John Ross, in the presence and hearing of Ms. Michelle Greenwood and other persons unknown to the plaintiff, spoke false and defamatory words concerning the plaintiff, the substance of which was that Mr. Li was ineffective in dealing with his subcontractors, was sloppy in his work, and routinely late in getting his work done.

After the discovery in this case, the record has been made clear on a number of facts:

1. Plaintiff and defendant are brothers-in-law;

2. Plaintiff and defendant are competitors; they are both general contractors.

3. The statements were made on July 11, YR-2, after the plaintiff had submitted a bid to renovate Ms. Greenwood's property into condominiums.

4. That after the July 11 conversation, Ms. Greenwood turned down the plaintiff's bid and hired the defendant to renovate this property into condominiums.

5. That the statements made by the defendant, Mr. Ross, if they were made at all, were limited to the statements made in the complaint. (Summary of Deposition of Mr. Greenwood, page 81 attached).

QUESTION PRESENTED

I. DID DEFENDANT'S STATEMENTS TO GREENWOOD AMOUNT TO SLANDER?

SHORT ANSWER

I. NO; DEFENDANT'S WORDS WERE MERELY STATEMENTS OF OPINION NOT AMOUNTING TO FIGHTING WORDS. SUCH WORDS ARE NOT DEFAMATORY NOR SLANDEROUS AND ARE PROTECTED UNDER THE FIRST AMENDMENT'S GUARANTEE OF FREE SPEECH.

A statement by a competitor in a commercial environment that he can undersell another and does better work is not defamatory per se since the recipient can only regard it as a relative statement of opinion, grounded on the speaker's obvious bias, and having no tendency other than to express the speaker's viewpoint. *See Chaves v. Johnson*, Nita 335 S.E.2d 97, 103 (Nita, YR-4).

In the *Chaves* case, a similar factual situation arose. One architect sued another for defamation after his competitor wrote a letter to his customer offering a lower fee and characterizing him as inexperienced and as charging excessive fees for the particular project involved. The court held such words were mere statements of opinion that did not impugn the plaintiff's character or professional standing. Pure expressions of opinion not amounting to fighting words cannot be the basis of defamation, the court held. Further, "the first amendment to the federal constitution and article 1, section 12 of the Constitution of Nita protect the right of the people to teach, preach, write, or speak any such opinion, however ill-founded, without inhibition by actions for libel and slander." *Chaves* at 102.

Clearly, the *Chaves* case is controlling in the present situation. The defendant's words are constitutionally protected expressions of the opinion that are necessary and appropriate in the commercial environment. These opinions did not impugn the plaintiff's character or professional standing. The defendant's opinions do not amount to defamation or slander, therefore plaintiff's motion for judgment on this cause of action, as well as his claim of tortious interference of the right of contract, should be stricken.

Nita's position on this is consistent with the Restatement 2d of Torts, § 566. *See also Gertz v. Robert Welch, Inc.*, 418 U.S. 323, 339 (1974) (where the Supreme Court held that as long as they do not impose liability without fault, the States may define for themselves the appropriate standard of liability for a publisher or broadcaster of defamatory falsehood injurious to a private individual); *cf. Milkovich v. Lorain Journal Co.*, 89-645, 58 LAW WEEK 4846 (1990) (where the U.S. Supreme Court ruled that the First Amendment does not prohibit application of state libel law to statements of opinion involving private figures that contain provably false factual connotations).

"Under the First Amendment there is no such thing as a false idea. However pernicious an opinion may seem we depend for its correction not on the conscience of judges and juries but on the competition of other ideas."

CONCLUSION

The defendant's actions amounted merely to acceptable business competition. There was no improper interference with plaintiff's right to contract. Defendant merely sought to divert prospective business from a competitor to himself. His words were neither defamatory nor slanderous, but rather constitutionally protected expressions of opinion.

Fred Smith

Fred Smith
Attorney for Defendant

CERTIFICATE OF SERVICE

I hereby certify that a true and exact copy of the above Motion to Strike and the accompanying Memorandum in Support of Motion to Strike was personally served on Mr. Harold Baker, Esq., counsel for the plaintiff, at Suite 1200, United Virginia Bank Building, Nita City, Nita 23219, on this the January 15 day of the YR-2.

Fred Smith

Fred Smith
Attorney for Defendant

IN THE CIRCUIT COURT OF NITA CITY, NITA

Doug Li, dba Li Builders,	)	
	)	
Plaintiff	)	**ORDER ON DEFENDANT'S**
	)	**MOTION FOR SUMMARY**
v.	)	**JUDGMENT PLAINTIFF'S**
	)	**SLANDER CLAIM**
John Ross and	)	
Ross Construction Co., Inc.	)	No. 1234
	)	
	)	
Defendants	)	

Defendant's Motion for Partial Summary Judgment to Plaintiff's Slander Claim for Relief is hereby granted. Under the authority of *Chaves v. Johnson*, 335 S.E.2d 97, 103 (Nita, YR-4), the context of the defendant's statements make the statements opinion, not defamation. This ruling, however, leaves intact the plaintiff's claims for interference with contract and interference with perspective advantage.

The jury permissibly might find that the defendant's statements when taken together with a showing that defendant indeed knew about a contract or a prospective economic advantage existing between the plaintiff and Ms. Greenwood, acted either with malice or that the defendant acted "improperly."

Dated this 15th day of January, YR-1, at Nita City, Nita.

Honorable John Carrington
_____

JUDGE, NITA CIRCUIT COURT

DEFENDANTS' CONFIDENTIAL MATERIALS

Initial Interview with John/Joan Ross[1]
November 30, YR-2

ADDRESS

Office   5411 Patterson Avenue

                        Nita City, Nita

Residence   8 Fairway Drive

                        Nita City, Nita

AGE   36

MARITAL STATUS   Wife, Martha Ross, married YR-11

                        Husband, Arthur Swanson, married YR-11

CHILDREN   Karen (8)

EDUCATION   BS, Princeton, YR-14

MILITARY SERVICE   None

PRESENT JOB   Chairman and CEO of Ross Construction Co., Inc.

I am a shareholder, chairman of the board, and chief executive officer of Ross Construction Co., Inc. I own 60 percent of the common stock; my mother owns 20 percent, and my sister, Mary, owns 20 percent. Ross Construction has been in existence for over forty years.

I was born and raised in Nita City. My family has lived in the Nita City area for over 150 years. Our family has owned a 1,000 acre farm down on the Old River for generations.

I have lived in Nita City most of my life, except for college and the Peace Corps. I went to St. Catherine's, a private school, for both elementary and high school. I first met my wife while I was in high school. We married after I returned from the Peace Corps.

I joined the business in YR-12, seven years before my father's death. I had just returned from a stint in the Peace Corps, where I did general contractor's work. I built cement block buildings for meeting halls, schools, and storage facilities. When I came back from Africa, I was made a job supervisor in Dad's business. I prepared bids, contracted with the subcontractors, supervised jobs, and did office work. Generally speaking, I learned the business. After Dad died, I took over the business and continued to do what I had done before, and, of course, took on greater responsibility for making day-to-day business decisions and broader financial investment decisions.

---

1. The transcript of Ross's interview was excerpted so that only the answers are reprinted here. Assume that this is a true and accurate rendering of those answers. This witness role can be played by a male or a female. Use the information provided accordingly.

I first met the plaintiff in this case, Li, at Princeton. I believe it was in my sophomore year. The plaintiff was a year behind me in school. We both debated. In fact, Li met my sibling at a debate competition. They married after their graduation. I had left for the Peace Corps the year before they got married and was not around when Dad offered Li a position with Ross Construction. I know I would have been against it. We didn't really get along in college. He hung out with a strange group of people. They were a group of real science and computer whizzes who seemed to look down their noses at others.

In addition, Li and I came to compete for the same spot on the debate team. We first met in an inter-school competition, which I won. We both made the team. Just before the meet against Harvard, just after I had a bout with the flu, Li was announced as a member of the team, and I became the alternate. I really felt I was treated badly by the coach and the team. Li had never worked at debating as hard as I had. He was only stronger because I had been ill and my strength was coming back day by day. I would have been fine for the debate. Li didn't seem to be too troubled by it all. He really played it up the day of the meet, and I have always resented his attitude that day.

When I returned from the Peace Corps, I found that Doug was in tight with my father. It was my opinion that Doug was dead weight around the business, and I told my father this on a number of occasions. I feel my father began to agree with me and that was why when my father died in YR-5 of a heart attack, the business was left entirely to me. No, I don't know whether Dad ever spoke to Doug directly about his inabilities, or how I felt. Doug left the business shortly thereafter of his own volition. Doug has been struggling along with his own general contracting business, mostly on small jobs, for the last few years.

My father had left my sister Mary with a considerable inheritance. I am convinced Doug is milking my sister's inheritance to get started in business. I know that Mary can't sell her stock without first offering it to the business, so Doug can't get at the inheritance directly, but I believe Mary has pledged the stock to secure a loan for a substantial sum of money.

I vaguely remember having a conversation with my sister around the time that Doug left the business. Doug had just given notice that he was leaving. It was only shortly after Dad had died, so it was an emotional time. Mary was upset that Doug was leaving, but I told her there was nothing I could do about it. I told her that it was probably for the best because I thought that Doug wanted to call his own shots and take his own chances. I don't remember calling Doug any names, but I may have. We were both pretty upset.

As to my dealings with Ms. Greenwood, I know that Ms. Greenwood had been a good friend of my father. She has told me she held my father in the highest regard. Though I'm not certain about this, I suspect that Doug had used my father's relationship with Ms. Greenwood to be in the running on this job in the first place.

I first found out about the renovation job in a conversation I had with Dave Peters. Dave is a subcontractor I do a lot of work with. Dave told me—on Wednesday, July 9—that he had been turned down by my brother-in-law, Doug, on a pretty big renovation project. He said that Doug must have been really moving up in the world. When I asked about the project, Dave told me it was Ms. Greenwood's Little Sisters of the Poor Convent condominium conversion project. This conversation started me thinking about the renovation business again. I had been planning to make a move in this area for some time, and this really sparked my interest. With all the energy credits and tax credits for historical renovation, there is real incentive to do historical renovations on a major scale. Condominium conversions are also a nice way to keep subcontractors busy between big jobs. I also don't have to deal with a lot of paperwork or with union contractors, or worry about federal and state work requirements in working on these jobs.

I decided to give Ms. Greenwood a call on Friday, July 11, YR-2. No, Dave did not tell me that Doug had already landed the job. He simply told me that Doug had turned his bid down, taking instead a bid from a competitor. I do remember he said something about being angry because he had rushed his bid—he said his bid was competitive—only to have it turned down. I don't treat subs that way. You have to really treat your subs right. I even take all my subcontractors out for a Christmas dinner, on me, just to tell them how much I appreciate the relationship.

In any event, when I heard that Ms. Greenwood was considering a renovation, I made a lunch appointment with her at the club (NCC) and convinced her that I was right for the job. I called Greenwood around mid-morning and spoke with her office manager, Goldstein. I don't remember anything Goldstein said to me other than that she connected me with Ms. Greenwood. No, I don't remember that she said anything about a contract with another general contractor. I told Ms. Greenwood who I was and asked her if I could meet her for lunch and discuss her renovation project. I suggested the Club. She told me she hadn't been to the Club in ages and that lunch there sounded great. We met for lunch around noon. I picked her up, and we rode out together. Our conversation on the way out was about family and golf games.

About the conversation concerning her renovation, I told her that Li didn't have the contacts in the area that I did, that he didn't have the leverage with subcontractors that the Ross name brought to a job, and that he didn't really have what it takes in the way of employees or management skills to do the quality job I knew Greenwood required. No, I don't think I ever said to Greenwood that Doug was late in getting things done. I don't know anything about Doug's timeliness since he left Ross Construction. I don't recall he had any problem being timely at Ross either, but Dad handled most of those situations if they arose. I do think I said I thought Doug was sloppy. I was describing his attitude toward his work. I stand behind each one of the statements I made.

I feel what really turned Greenwood to me was my track record on the major construction jobs. Sure, I'll save her money on this job. No, I won't be under 25 million for the total cost, but that is because of all the changes that have been required since I first started. They've all been approved by Ms. Greenwood or the owners of the individual units. Doug would have been even more expensive, I'm sure.

I did know that Doug had put together some plans and submitted a bid, but I didn't know for sure if the contract had actually been signed. I remember Greenwood hesitated when I told her I could save her some money. I asked her whether she had signed a thirty- to forty-page standard form agreement. She told me she hadn't. I told her that then she wasn't bound on anything, and I guaranteed that she could switch. Ross Construction Company (and all reputable contractors I know) uses AIA form agreements.

I have never been arrested or convicted of anything.

I'm in arbitration concerning contracting. Ross Construction is in arbitration about twice a year, on the average. Most of the problems deal with cost overruns or not getting paid. We haven't been sued for missing an outside deadline in the last five years.

Though the attached financial statements show Ross Construction's net assets at about $20 million, I would say that the true value of the company is closer to $100 million. I certainly wouldn't sell the company for any less than that.

I belong to the Nita Country Club and have been recently named chair of the membership committee. In the past the Nita Country Club has discriminated against Asians, Blacks, and Jews. I am opposed to discrimination, but I don't think I have the votes to change the policy. Actually I don't think it's anybody's business and would rather not answer questions about it if I don't have to.

Initial Interview with Mike/Michelle Greenwood[1]

December 29, YR-2

ADDRESS	2445 River Road Drive
	Nita City, Nita
AGE	40
MARITAL STATUS	Husband, Bradley, YR-17
	Wife, Jody, YR-17
CHILDREN	Sidney (13)
EDUCATION	BA, University of Nita, YR-18
MILITARY SERVICE	None
PRESENT JOB	Developer/CEO/Chairperson of the Board of Area Corporation

I have been involved in the business since I graduated from the University of Nita about eighteen years ago. I took over the business from my father twelve years ago. My family is a sixth-generation Nita City family. Before my family went into real estate, they were long-time landowners in Nita, down on the Old River. My family still owns a good deal of this land. I now live at 2445 River Road Drive, Nita City, Nita.

The Area Corporation is a small development corporation with eleven full-time employees. Goldstein used to be the vice president for operations. As of last week I have a new one, Bernie Seigel. The office manager oversees the work of three salespeople, two researchers, and five secretaries. We purchase land and buildings with an eye toward improving the property with housing or condominiums. Recently I've been concentrating on historical renovations in downtown areas.

We do have an office procedure for handling both the telephone and dealing with correspondence. It worked the same when Goldstein was the office manager:

1. I or Goldstein—now, Seigel—will dictate a letter on the Dictaphone or e-mail with an attached Word document, a draft of the letter.

2. Our secretaries transcribe the letter in rough form, or, in the case of an e-mail, format the attached Word document on our letterhead and place it in our "In" box. Goldstein, Seigel, and I prefer to work off a hard copy.

3. We correct it and make any additions or deletions on the hard copy and put it in our "Out" boxes.

---

1. The transcript of Greenwood's interview was excerpted so that only the answers are reprinted here. Assume that this is a true and accurate rendering of those answers. This witness role can be played by a male or a female. Use the information provided accordingly.

4. Our secretaries pick it up and incorporate our changes into the document, make a copy, and put it in the "In" box. They also type an envelope and paper clip it to the original and copy of the letter.

5. We make any corrections necessary, in which case we call and our secretaries make the changes. If no changes are needed, we sign it and put it in the envelope. Then we put it in the "Out" box.

6. Our secretaries pick up signed originals, fold it, put it in the envelope, and run them through the postage meter. They deposit the stamped letters in the U.S. mailbox on their coffee break at 10:00 a.m. The mail is picked up at 10:15 a.m. from the mailbox. Goldstein also often went to the mailbox on his/her way home at 5:30 p.m. (for afternoon mail).

7. A hard copy of the letter is placed by me (or by my direction) in the file under the name of the addressee. Ms. Goldstein (now Siegel) and I (and our secretaries) are the only people who have access to the files.

The procedure for incoming calls is as follows:

1. They always answer the phone the same way, "Area Corporation, may I help you?"

2. If the party asks for me, the secretaries and Goldstein asked for their name and the purpose of their call.

3. The secretaries or Goldstein asked them to hold while they check for me (or for Goldstein, if the secretaries answered and I was not there).

4. The secretaries would buzz me, as did Goldstein, on the intercom and tell me (or Goldstein, as the case may be), who was calling and for what purpose.

5. The party was either connected with me (or Goldstein) or the secretaries or Goldstein took a message.

6. If the secretaries or Goldstein took a message, it was usually on a "phone-o-gram" message form, though sometimes they might just e-mail me if they thought it was particularly important. (I am starting to access my messages more and more by checking my e-mail.) They kept a copy of the message (or file a copy of their e-mail) and the original went to me. If it was a phone-o-gram, the copies are in a large spiral binder book that Goldstein supervised. When one ran out, approximately every three weeks, Goldstein filed the filled book for future reference. I don't know what Goldstein did with e-mails, but I assume she kept an electronic copy of all e-mails she sent me.

I believe that I first met the parties to this lawsuit through their father, John Ross Sr., and I sat on the Board of Directors of the Nita Museum. I also had heard of Ross Construction and the work the Ross Construction Company had done on the River Road Baptist Church, on the Davenport Museum, and on a number of other major construction projects in and around Nita City. I believe I also met Li one time when Doug and his father-in-law were having lunch in an establishment that I was also dining in—I think it was the Bull or Bear Club. Li and I had a long discussion about historical renovation. I remember that I got the impression that Li had the major responsibility for a number of Ross's projects and made a mental note to contact him if I ever looked to change general contractors. In any event, after I saw my architect's preliminary drawings, I somehow thought of Li's name and asked the architect to get in contact with him. I had just had a falling out with my previous general contractor. I never have bid my projects. I just try to get comfortable with a supervisor/general contractor and involve him throughout.

Mr. Johnson, the architect on the project, had been referred to me by my uncle. Johnson had designed some renovations on my uncle's home and came highly recommended. I was frankly disappointed with Johnson's initial drafting and suggested that he work more closely with the builder to formalize the plans and specifications for the additions and renovations. I recall asking Johnson to get hold of Li. I also recall telling Johnson that I knew Li and was convinced he would be a good general contractor for the job. I called Li myself and told him that Johnson would be getting in touch with him. I believe I called Li about June 28 or 29, YR-2 (I remember that it was shortly before the Fourth of July holiday). I also suggested that Li come out and see the convent and make a walk-through with me. We talked about what things we expected would have to be done. He met me at the convent that same afternoon. We did a walk-through, and he took notes on a note pad. I remember telling him that I wasn't really concerned so much about saving money as I was about having the work done right. My idea was that there was and is a real demand for quality downtown condominiums for the up-and-coming professionals. I did ask for a real rough estimate about the costs, and he told me it would be somewhere in the neighborhood of 20 to 25 million. I told him that 25 million sounded a bit high, and he assured me that he would do a very good job, a high-quality job, at a price that I was comfortable with. He told me he would get with the architect and get some bids in from some subcontractors and get back with me by the end of the week. He would also work closely with the architect on the blueprints, because I had mentioned my concern with Johnson's work. I recall him saying that it was his experience that the architects didn't really carefully consider some of the costs and building problems until they met with the builder. I remember assuring him that I fully expected that he would be able to do a high-quality job for me and that he had a good reputation—that Nita City certainly knew about Ross Construction.

It was then that he informed me that he was no longer with Ross Construction. I had not noticed this since my secretary had gotten me his number. He was obviously not listed under the same number as Ross Construction. Li explained to me that ever since he entered the building business twelve years before, he was very interested in doing historical renovation and that Ross Construction hadn't been going in that direction. He said he left Ross about four years ago and had developed a niche for himself in the renovation business. I don't remember being concerned at this time about Li not being with Ross Construction. He seemed like a very capable and confident contractor and gave me no reasons to doubt his abilities. In fact, it seemed an advantage to me that he was not with Ross Construction. He would then not be sidetracked by other major construction projects. It was his experience with Ross that I was more interested in, more than who he presently worked with. After all, he would really be working for me if things worked out.

It was on Friday, July 11, that next week after the Fourth, that I got a call from his brother-in-law, John Ross. John invited me out to lunch that day at the Nita Country Club. (I had not been out to the Club for a number of weeks and thought it might be a good chance to catch up with some old friends.) John Ross told me what prompted his calling—that he had heard that I was doing a condo conversion on the convent and that he might be able to give me a better deal than I was getting elsewhere. He did not say, nor did I ask, who told him about the project. I told him I would be happy to talk to him about it and get his advice. I believe it was a Friday noon that we met at the Club, and we had a very pleasant lunch. After catching up on his family and his golf game, he asked me about the project. After I described the renovations, Ross asked me what price I was getting. I told him I had reviewed Doug's bid and that it was around 25 million—but the price would obviously vary as construction progressed and the various individual buyers' needs were considered. He told me that he thought the price was too high and that if I would let him do the renovation, he would guarantee me a 10 percent savings. He told me that he had more experience than his brother-in-law in the industry, that he had more leverage with the subcontractors because of the big jobs he was involved in, and that he had heard that Doug had been having some trouble finishing jobs on time. I also recall that he said something about how Doug could be sloppy in his work, at least when he worked for Ross Sr.

I told John that while I hesitated at switching general contractors at this late date, I wasn't one to throw money away, and if he could save me 10 percent-plus on the job and guarantee me the same quality, then I might go with him. He asked me about whether I had signed anything with Li. I believe that I hesitated. I don't remember that I said that I signed something, but I might have. He then asked me whether I had signed any thirty- to forty-page document called the "American Institute of Architects Standard Form Agreement Between Owner and Contractor." I told him I didn't recall such a document, and didn't believe that I had. John then said it was no problem if I wanted to switch over and come with him. I still hesitated. Then he said, "Look, I guarantee that it's all right to switch. It happens all the time in the construction industry."

The reason I hesitated was that on the earlier Tuesday evening, July 8, Li had delivered to me the blueprints that he and the architect had worked up along with an indication of the overall cost of the project. I hadn't gotten the plans until Thursday. I had looked over the plans with my spouse on Thursday night and on Friday morning, before John's call setting up lunch. I told my operations manager that we were excited about the plans and specifications for the renovations. I had told my secretary Friday morning to notify Doug that I had approved the plans and specifications and the estimate that he had submitted. My secretary told me she would get a note out to him to that effect that morning.

Regarding the July 11 letter, I'm not sure that that's my signature. It could be Goldstein's signature. I may have told Goldstein to prepare the letter and sign it for me. In any event, I would have allowed Goldstein to sign the letter in order to get it out on time. I've done that before.

When I got back from my lunch with John, I asked my secretary whether she had sent the note to Doug. She told me she had. I asked Goldstein to make sure and Goldstein checked and the letter was gone. I asked Goldstein to call Li's office and leave a message that he should disregard the prior note and that I was debating as to what to do. I know Goldstein didn't get through because she received a call late on Monday from Li and had to tell him that I had decided to go with someone else. Earlier that same Monday, about 10:00 a.m., John had stopped by the office to look at the plans and specs that Doug had drawn up with the architect. I expressed some discomfort at giving him Doug's plans and bids. He told me that the plans were the architect's plans and that he would work with Johnson if I was satisfied with them. Once more, Ross told me switching contractors happened all the time—that contractors came and went, but architects' plans are the owner's. He promised I'd have no problems going with him. I hadn't much experience with switching contractors since I have only worked with one general contractor up to that point in my business. Ross had also looked over Li's bid and assured me that he could save me about $2.5 million by lowering the subcontractors' prices and not do anything to the quality of the work that was to be done. I didn't feel real comfortable switching, but with the assurances as to quality, the lower price, and the earlier allusions to the quality and trustworthiness of Doug's work, I decided to go with Ross. The decision was strictly a business decision on my part.

The work on the show units was supposed to be completed by November 1, YR-2, but Ross instead completed the work in December YR-2. I am a bit disappointed in the timeliness of their performance, but Ross seems to be doing a good job, and from all appearances, the renovation will look as we planned it. I don't think the fact that I'm in an ongoing relationship with Ross affects any of the things that I am saying. I have not seen any of Li's work after he left Ross Construction.

I had a conversation with Li at a wedding a couple of months after I switched contractors. He was really upset. I told him what Ross had said to me at the country club. When Li became even more upset I backed out of the conversation, and told him I didn't want to get involved in the family squabbles. It was strictly a business decision as far as I was concerned.

I'm not opposed to considering Li as a contractor in the future, if that would help things. I just got nervous about Li after talking to Ross and was convinced Ross could do a better job and save me some money. I'm not sure why Goldstein left. She gave me notice late December, last year. I really miss her. She was more important to my business than I realized . . . and it's always tough to train someone new. The new person is getting better each day, but seven years of experience are hard to make up in a short time.

I think Goldstein left because she received better benefits at her new job.

I did invite Goldstein to the Club one day shortly before she left. She was going to take notes on my discussions with Ross about the Old Towne development. I forgot and made reservations in the members-only dining room. When I got there and they wouldn't seat us, we decided to sit in the lounge. Goldstein was a little upset and said she would just go back to the office.

I apologized when I got back. She accepted my apology, and I thought nothing more about it. Then she gave me a week's notice and quit.

The Old Towne project is a renovation of about fifteen eighteenth-century homes in Old Towne Nita that I picked up for a song. The structures are solid, but there needs to be major renovations, and the important thing will be to preserve their historical character. I'm expecting that they will sell for around 2 million apiece when they are completed. We are still just getting the plans approved for the individual renovations. These approvals have been tricky and much more involved than I anticipated. Johnson is the architect. John Ross told me that he did not have the interest in the Old Towne project, so I'm looking for a new contractor.

Initial Interview with Dave/Darleen Peters[1]

December 10, YR-2

ADDRESS	2206 Curving Fair Drive
	Nita City, Nita
AGE	57
MARITAL STATUS	Wife, Ricki, married YR-25
	Husband, Richard, married YR-25
CHILDREN	Dale (22), David (20)
EDUCATION	High School Diploma
MILITARY SERVICE	Army
PRESENT JOB	Carriers Air Conditioning and Heating

My two children are grown. I've lived in Nita City all my life, except for my army days. I'm a high school graduate.

I now work for Carriers Air Conditioning and Heating. I've worked there for four years. Before that I worked as a general contractor for Thalhimer's. I worked my way up into a supervisory position, overseeing all of their construction. I worked for Thalhimer's for twenty-eight years. I supervised the building of seven of their stores in and around Nita City and also supervised countless renovations of existing stores.

I have been very active in the Association of Nita City General Contractors. I am a past secretary, vice president, and president of the association. I have put on educational meetings for contractors. I have lobbied on their behalf in the Nita General Assembly. The association serves the needs of all licensed general contractors in Nita City. I continue to be a member of the association.

I left Thalhimer's because I ran into some health problems. I had a heart attack and took early retirement. I found retirement impossible, so I went back to work at Carriers part-time. I do bids for Carriers. I was familiar with their product and had connections in the industry, so they were eager to hire me, even if I can only work part-time.

I've known Ross and Ross Sr. for many years. They were involved in building two of the Thalhimer stores. I worked primarily with Ross Sr., though I did become acquainted with both Ross Jr., and Li's work. They were both qualified and able contractors. I had no complaints with their work.

Recently I've done a good deal of Ross's air-conditioning and heating work. I would guess we've sold over one million dollars' worth of air-conditioning units for Ross jobs in the last year. I'm a salaried employee

---

1. The transcript of Peters's interview was excerpted so that only his answers are reprinted here. Assume that this is a true and accurate rendering of those answers. This witness role can be played by a male or a female. Use the information provided accordingly.

at Carrier's—I make about $75,000 a year part-time. Carrier's' markup on their product runs from twenty to twenty-five percent.

I was first contacted about the Greenwood job by Li. It was in early July, the Monday after the Fourth, that I got a call for a rush bid on the Greenwood condominium conversion. I ran out that same day (I remember I came across town against rush hour traffic and stayed late preparing the bid). I found out on Tuesday that Doug had turned me down even though there was no difference between my price and York's. I was more than a little upset that I got turned down. It didn't seem like good business to ask someone to do a rush job favor so you can look good, then arbitrarily turn you down.

On Wednesday, I ran into Ross on another job site. He and I were involved in some work on the federal court building downtown. I mentioned to him that I was bugged at Li and the way he handled my bid. He asked me what Li was working on. I told him that the job was to renovate the Little Sisters of the Poor Convent. I don't remember exactly what he said, but he expressed empathy with my situation; something like, "Well, what do you expect from someone who was not raised right . . . you know . . . who is not from here?" No, I didn't take that as a racist comment; Ross was just expressing an attitude that many have here in Nita, that people from Nita are just more civil to each other, less cut throat, and more genteel. I didn't know at that time that he was planning to compete with Doug for the Greenwood job. I do know that I told him it was a rush job and that I had been turned down the day before.

Sure, I thought I was talking to someone sympathetic to my problem. Yes, I did know that Ross and Li had a falling out. I'd heard it had something to do with Li's . . . well, I'm not sure I'd better repeat it since I don't know who I heard it from or how reliable the information was. Suffice it to say, I knew Ross and Li had problems and were not working together. The next week, when Ross called and asked me to join his bid on the same project, I agreed to cut my bid by about 10 percent. I believe Ross suggested it. I figured that I had already sunk five hours in the bid. Besides, Ross is a big customer and the future business is important.

From my experience with the contracting business over the last twenty-eight years I have never had a contract with someone for more than $50,000 that wasn't on some version of the Architect's Standard Form Contract. I have contracted on behalf of Thalhimer's for jobs as large as $40 million and as small as $500. I am aware that some small jobs are contracted for on the back of napkins, but, in my opinion, it is reasonable for Ross to believe that a contract this large would be formed on a standard form contract. On the jobs the size that Ross Construction does, I'd be surprised if they ever contracted without using an Architect Standard Form contract of some sort. Oh, maybe Ross Sr. didn't require a contract eight to ten years ago, but it certainly is customary in the building industry to have one today.

No, I've never done any work with Li.

Yes, I also have an opinion on whether Li would have made any money if he worked with Greenwood. Though I think his pricing is in the ball park, more importantly I think he was in over his head and would have run into difficulties. Also, a number of other things make Li's claim for damages questionable. First, it is very possible that Greenwood would switch general contractors in mid-job if she was dissatisfied with Li's work. It happens all the time. Second, it is my opinion that Greenwood would most likely use an Old Towne general contractor to do her project there. I always found in working for Thalhimer's that knowledge of the local subcontractors was crucial to doing a job right. Transporting subs from Nita City would raise costs too high. That's why, in my opinion, Greenwood would probably go with an Old Towne general contractor on the Old Towne job.

Initial Interview with Bob/Bette Johnson[1]
October 15, YR-2

ADDRESS	2108 Fairview Court
	Nita City, Nita
AGE	35
MARITAL STATUS	Wife, Leah, married YR-11
	Husband, Doug, married YR-11
CHILDREN	None
EDUCATION	BA, University of Michigan, YR-12
	MA, University of Michigan, YR-9
MILITARY SERVICE	None
PRESENT JOB	Architect

I went to U of Michigan, started in engineering, switched to art, and ended up with a bachelor's degree in architecture. I then worked for an architectural firm in Detroit, doing drafting for the building of pizza parlors. After two years in Detroit, I went back to U of M and got my master's in architecture. I went to work for a big firm in Iowa City, Iowa. My wife and I started to miss family and friends who had since moved to Nita, so we moved to Nita City after two years in Iowa City.

After moving to Nita City, I joined a small firm. I have since left and gone out on my own. I've been on my own for about five years now. I've mostly been doing historical renovation work, though I've just been offered a major job designing an office complex for Central Fidelity Bank. I am a member of the Nita City Historical Society. I'm starting to get a lot of work in this area.

You're really putting me in a tough spot by asking me these questions. I have nothing against either of these guys, and I hope to do work for both of them in the future. I got called into this by Ms. Greenwood. She had heard good things about work I had done for Greenwood's uncle—I take particular pains to design an addition that doesn't look like an addition. I made some preliminary drafts for Greenwood, but told her that my experience had been that it was often helpful to work with a builder in designing a renovation like this. I asked her if she had someone in mind to be general contractor or whether I might recommend someone. She mentioned Li, and I said I had heard of him. I really didn't know his work; I had only heard his name mentioned as someone involved in home renovation. No, I hadn't heard anything negative about Li's work. I know he had worked for a number of years for Ross, so I assume he knows what he is doing. He was very capable, precise, and comprehensive in putting the bid together.

---

1. The transcript of Johnson's interview was excerpted so that only the answers are reprinted here. Assume that this is a true and accurate rendering of those answers. This witness role can be played by a male or a female. Use the information provided accordingly.

In any event, Greenwood said she would call Li and tell him I would be getting up with him in the next couple of days. She said she would like something formalized by the Fourth of July. Li and I met off and on a number of days, I believe it was the two weeks before the Tuesday of the week after the Fourth. Li submitted my blueprints and his bid that Tuesday evening. I didn't know anything else until the next week when I called Greenwood and was told that Ross would be the general contractor.

I didn't say anything to Greenwood about this. It was none of my business. I was surprised by the switch, though such switches happen, even in mid-project. I really believed from what Greenwood said about Li earlier, and from the fact that Li was her suggestion, that Li was going to be the general contractor. Greenwood's approach up to this point had also suggested she wasn't shopping the bid. The time Li and I spent working up the bid led us to believe Li had it. No, I can't remember, specifically, anything that was said. I knew that we had worked hard to get the bid together and that Li seemed to really want it. Li was very concerned that he price it right for Greenwood. He told me he thought that this was a chance to get the credibility for these big renovations. I remember I had encouraged him to make sure he got his fair share, not to sell himself short. I remember urging him to go on a cost-plus-percentage basis rather than on a fixed-cost basis. I believe the standard percentage for cost-plus is about 10 percent. I think he went on that basis.

Ross priced his on a cost-plus basis. This is the only way to realistically do the project. Li's bid really is just a ballpark figure, and both Li and Greenwood knew that. Li was just giving some cost breakdowns on a per-foot basis and on a per-unit basis so that Greenwood would have at least some idea of the costs.

Yes, I recognize this document you've given me as the bid we worked up together. I don't see why Doug would have had any problem making his profit. These are all reputable subs, and they all usually stick by their estimates.

Yes, I am familiar with this form. This is an AIA standard form contract. I've been using this form, or some AIA form, on all my jobs. The AIA prepares this form as a way of standardizing the risks between architect, owner, and general contractor. It's a very useful document. You folks are the lawyers. I really don't know whether it's necessary to have an AIA before the parties are bound. All I know is that I always use them.

In the end, Ross may indeed be cheaper. Ross may take advantage of some long-term deal with the subs to get them to give him a discount.

We've been having a little problem with timely performance on the renovation—maybe a little more so than usual. Subs are often tied up longer than they projected on other jobs and have trouble coordinating efforts. Some of that is to be expected. A couple of Ross's subs have been tied up on other jobs with Ross—but I'm sure it will not put the project in ultimate jeopardy. These things happen all the time in construction. I don't enjoy that part of the business—dealing with owner expectations that work will be done on time and meshing these with the contractor's need to finish other projects and plan for new ones. I guess that's why there are contractors and there are architects. All I'm doing now is making sure the construction conforms to the design specs or that the substitution is acceptable. I visit the site on the average of about once every week.

DOCUMENTS AVAILABLE TO BOTH SIDES

Plaintiff's Exhibits

DOUG LI, GENERAL CONTRACTOR

3455 SINKING LINE DRIVE

NITA CITY, NITA 23222

(804) 321-2133

July 8, YR-2

Michelle Greenwood
Area Corporation
800 Main Street
Nita City, Nita 23219

Re: Warsaw Condominium Project

Dear Ms. Greenwood:

Per your request, I have estimated the cost to construct condominiums at the Warsaw. I propose to complete construction for a total cost of $24,769,235. These costs exclude the cost of the major structural overhaul of the chapel, roofing, exterior brick work, and the landscaping which you have indicated you will supervise personally. My cost does include the condominium conversions in the chapel once the new floors and structural supports are in place, as we have discussed. My costs were developed as follows:

Direct Construction Costs

Main convent building offices and common areas	$19,994,000
Proposal fee	4,900
Subtotal	19,998,900
Overhead @ 10%	1,999,890
Profit @ 10%	1,999,890
Site Supervision and Support	170,555
Total	$24,769,235

Included herewith as part of this proposal is my scope outline, cost summary, and unit price schedule. As we discussed, due to the age of the building, you may be required to address additional repairs to conform with the building code for new construction. Some of these areas are addressed with my proposal because they represent good construction practice. Other concerns were simply beyond our scope. Following is an outline of major items I have come across in my review.

Electrical
Included in my scope. I will replace all existing fuse boxes with circuit breakers. Each service will be grounded properly. New wiring will conform to code.

Plumbing

My scope calls for replacement of damaged pipe. Gas piping will also be replaced and added with a value at each user location per code.

Fire Egress

Upstairs end units do not have a second means of egress. This is not addressed in our proposal.

My cost estimates include the following major assumptions that significantly add to the costs involved. Solid wood doors, wood frame windows, site-made as opposed to pre-manufactured kitchen cabinets, custom counter tops, double sinks, top-of-the-line appliances (including Viking ranges), built-in bookshelves, entrance foyer with quarried stone, hardwood floors, brick fireplaces, Italian tile in the bathrooms, pedestal wash basins, double jacuzzis, and special molding throughout.

My cost estimates also include a $2,050,000 estimate to cover common-area renovations, including the recreation area (pool shell and building and common plumbing, electricity, curbs and sidewalks, etc.). This amount was distributed among the units on a per-square-foot basis. I estimate approximately $560,000 for common plumbing and electricity; $50,000 for concrete work, including pool shell; and approximately $200,000 for the other common area work, including awnings, fire pump, Jockey pump, elevator, carpet in the public areas, pool deck, tile, pool filter, pool electrical, pool building heat pump, electrical heating, toilet, sauna, and pool kitchen appliances. As per our conversation, this estimate leaves out roof work, gutter work, security system work, fencing, or parking lot paving.

Ms. Greenwood, I am very pleased to be able to work with you on this project. I am prepared to start whenever you say and estimate I will be able to get the show units completed within six months of your notifying me that you are ready. I look forward to hearing from you concerning my estimate.

Sincerely,

Doug Li

Doug Li
Li Builders

List of Subs Who Have Given Estimates

Masonry   Perrin

Millwork   Beckstoffer & Sons

Painting   Sutton Bros.

HVAC   York

Plumbing   Peyronnet

Electrical Mills Elect.

Plaintiff's Exhibit 2

Note from the author: These architectural drawings are not in the materials to raise any factual or legal issues but are meant to give the reader a picture of the overall scope of the project.

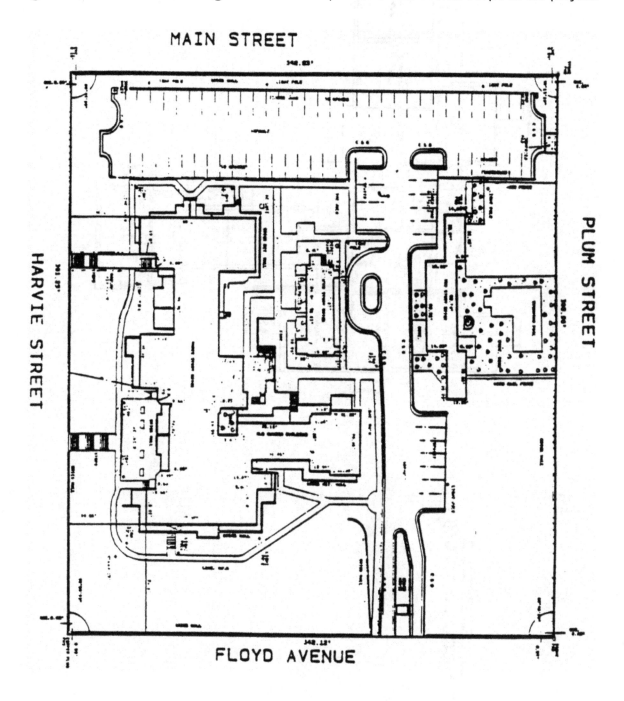

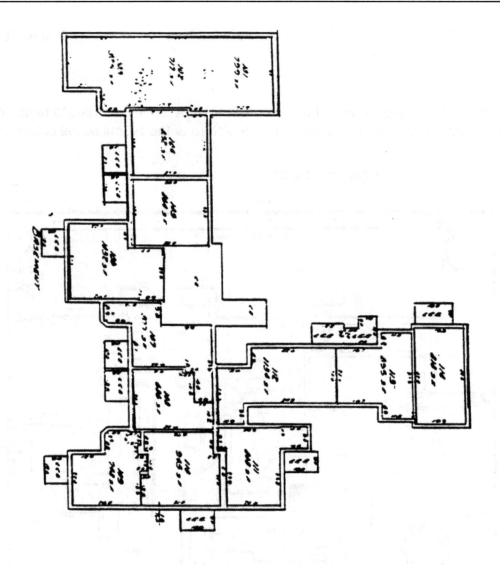

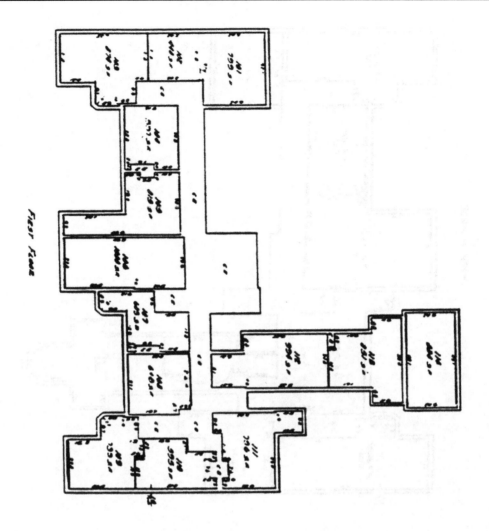

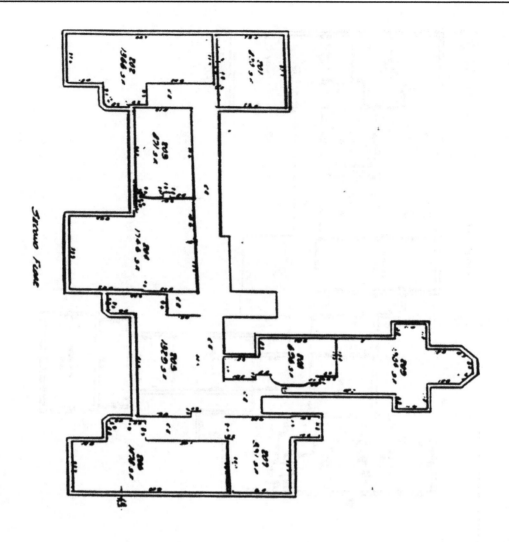

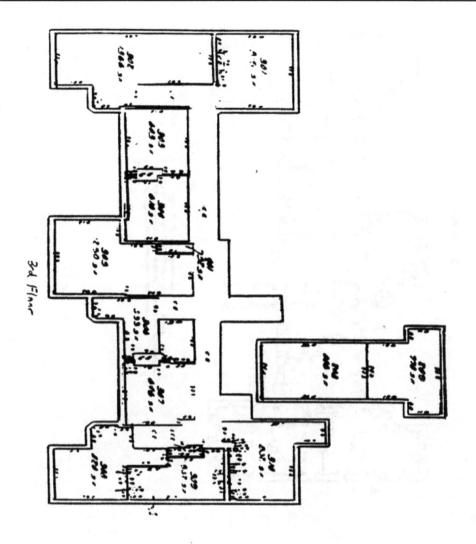

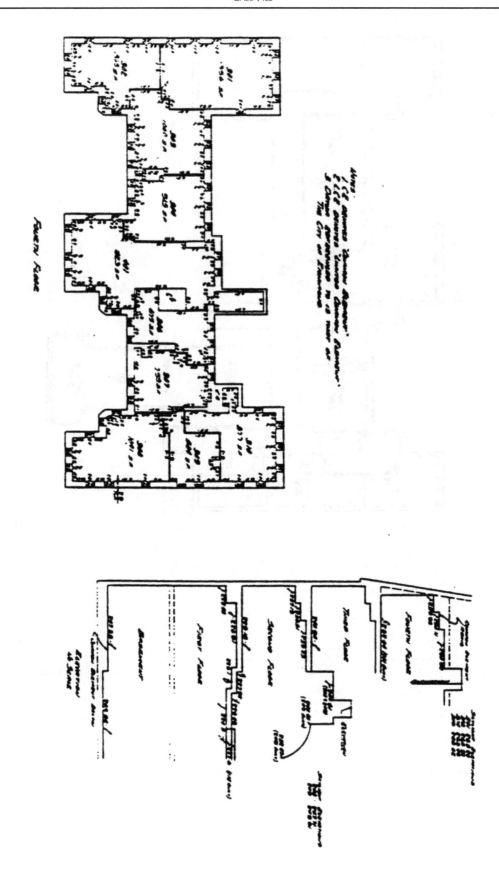

National Institute for Trial Advocacy

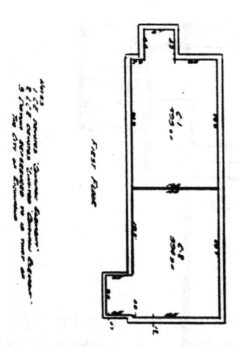
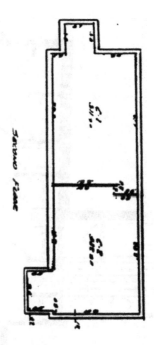

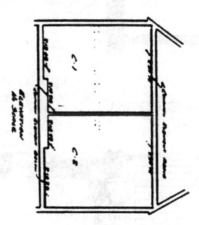

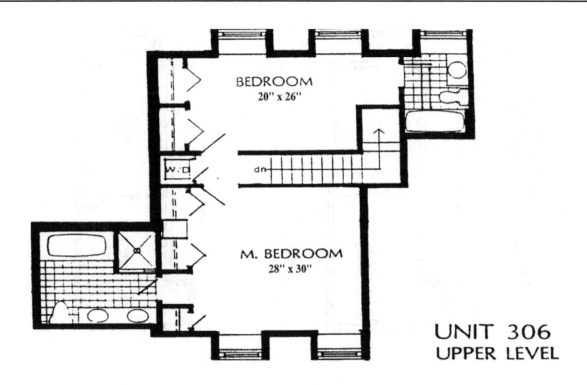

UNIT 306
UPPER LEVEL

BEDROOM
20" x 26"

M. BEDROOM
28" x 30"

dn

W/D

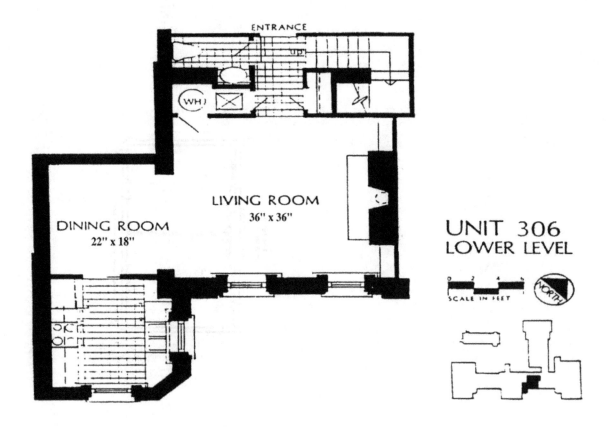

ENTRANCE

UP

WH

LIVING ROOM
36" x 36"

DINING ROOM
22" x 18"

UNIT 306
LOWER LEVEL

SCALE IN FEET

NORTH

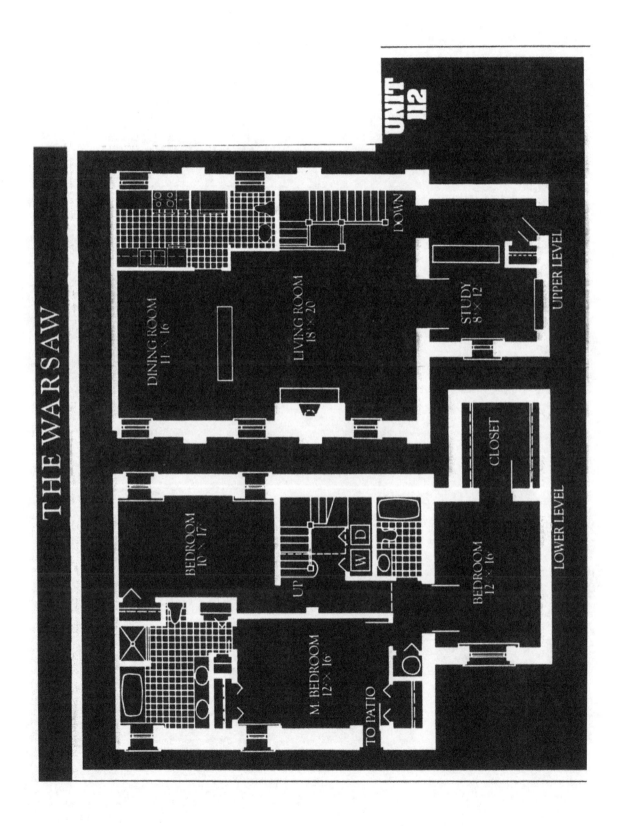

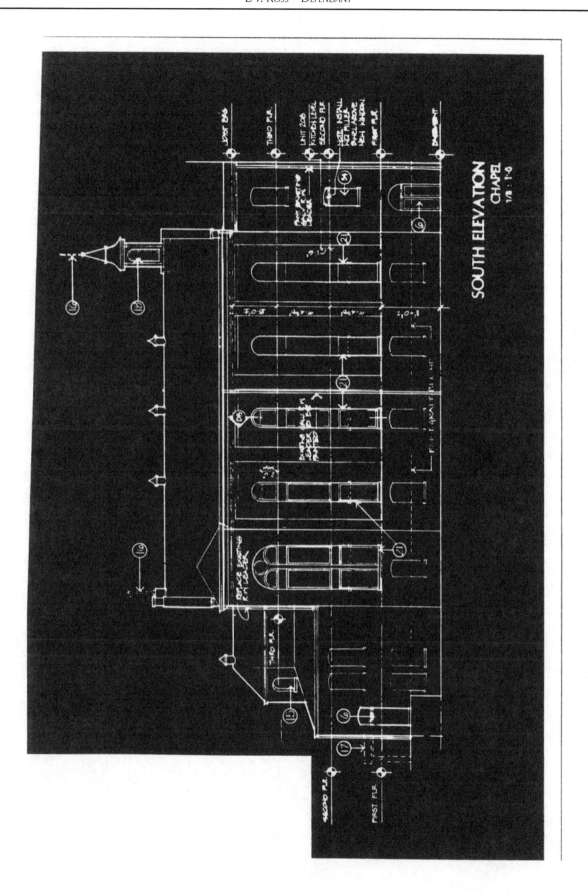

Estimate of Cost/Unit

Unit (Unit No.)	Gross Area (Square Feet)	Estimated Cost of Conversion
101	2,598	$580,000
102	2,157	420,000
103	2,699	616,000
104	2,449	520,600
105	2,679	610,000
106	3,112	766,000
107	2,482	540,000
108	2,334	484,000
109	2,487	540,000
110	2,540	560,000
111	2,604	582,000
112	3,128	772,000
113	2,706	620,000
114	2,702	618,000
C1	2,206	438,000
C2	2,176	420,000
201	1,820	298,000
202	2,366	496,000
203	1,871	316,000
204	2,746	634,000
205	2,329	482,000
206	2,478	536,000
207	1,831	302,000
208	2,582	574,000
209	3,082	756,000
301	3,171	788,000
302	3,231	810,000
303	2,603	582,000
304	2,525	554,000
305	2,250	454,000

Unit (Unit No.)	Gross Area (Square Feet)	Estimated Cost of Conversion
306	2,308	474,000
307	2,405	510,000
308	2,861	676,000
309	2,066	388,000
310	2,679	610,000
401	2,823	662,000
TOTAL	90,086	$19,994,000
Proposal Fee		4,900
		$19,998,900
+ 10% Profit		1,999,890
TOTAL		$21,998,790

Estimate for Two-Bedroom Condominium

Kitchen

Custom cabinets (see millwork below)	$ —
Appliances	$25,000
Double sink w/disposal	$ 1,500
Custom granite counters	$15,000
Water heater	$ 700

Bathroom

Toilet	$ 700
Jacuzzi	$10,000
Double sink	$ 600
Mirror	$ 600
Tile (see Italian tile below)	$ —
Shower stall	$ —
Dry Wall/Plastering (depends on square footage & layout)	$40,000–$100,000
Doors—Interior	$ 4,000
Doors—Exterior	$ 3,000
Marble Entrance	$10,000 - $30,000
Masonry/Fireplace	$20,000
Insulation	$ 5,000
Millwork: molding, cabinets (depends on square footage and layout), bookshelves, closet & shelves	$30,000–$70,000
Millwork: labor (for the above)	$10,500–$50,000

Hardwood flooring (depends on exact square footage and layout)	$10,500
Italian floor tile/ shower tile/Jacuzzi tile	$30,000
Interior paint/caulk	$10,000
Toilet accessories	$ 1,400
Final cleaning	$ 3,000
Plumbing	$10,000
Heat/AC	$20,200
Electrical	$20,300

Plaintiff's Exhibit 5

From: Michelle.Greenwood@AreaCorp.nita

To: DougLi@LiBuilders.nita

Date sent: 6/23/YR-2

Subject: Renovation project

Copies to:

Priority:

Are you interested in a major renovation condo conversion project? Can you meet this afternoon? If I don't hear from you, I'll try back.

Talk to you soon, Michelle

Plaintiff's Exhibit 6

From: MichelleGreenwood@AreaCorp.nita

To: DougLi@LiBuilders.nita

Date sent: 7/9/YR-2

Subject:

Copies to:

Priority:

Thanks for your prompt work with Johnson. I will get back on Friday. Thanks again,

Michelle

Plaintiff's Exhibit 7

From: office@AreaCorp.nita

To: DougLi@LiBuilders.nita

Date sent: 7/11/YR-2

Subject:

Copies to: MichelleGreenwood@AreaCorp.nita

Priority:

Please disregard the letter dated today. Another bid is being considered.

If you need to reach Ms. Greenwood, feel free to give her a call at 516-750-3922.

Cordially,

Abigail/Abe Goldstein
Vice President for Operations Area Corporation
800 Main Street
Nita City, Nita 23219

Plaintiff's Exhibit 8

AREA CORPORATION
800 MAIN STREET
NITA CITY, NITA 23219

MICHELLE GREENWOOD

July 11, YR-2

Mr. Doug Li
3455 Sinking Line Drive Nita City, Nita 23222

Dear Doug:

I looked over the plans and your estimate last night, and I am pleased to have you as general contractor to renovate the Little Sisters of the Poor Convent. Like I discussed with you before, I believe your early involvement helps the architect with his plans. The project seems to be coming together nicely.

I now plan to take Johnson's work and get major structural work roofing, etc., started. I will contact you as soon as we need plumbing and electrical work and as soon as we can start on the individual units. I would like to have the show units ready by November 1, YR-2.

Sincerely,

Michelle Greenwood

Michelle Greenwood

MG/ag

Plaintiff's Exhibit 9

ARCHITECT'S REPORT

THE WARSAW CONDOMINIUMS

16 N. Harvie Street
Nita City, Nita 23220

PRESENT CONDITION OF THE CONDOMINIUM AND
REPLACEMENT REQUIREMENTS FOR COMMON ELEMENTS

BOB JOHNSON, ARCHITECT
17 East Main Street
Nita City, Nita 23223

REPLACEMENT REQUIREMENTS FOR COMMON ELEMENTS AT THE WARSAW

When newly constructed, the normal life of housing units similar in type to these should be thirty-five years or more. In this project, the renovations are so extensive that these units would have to be evaluated as new units, with no depreciation.

The useful life of items shown in the following pages is an expected useful life expressly conditioned on standard usage and normal periodic maintenance. The gutters and roof, for example, need periodic maintenance and periodic coating of water-proofing materials. The pool and pool equipment useful life expectancy is also determined by the quality and type of daily maintenance provided in keeping the correct chemical balances in the water, equipment maintenance, etc. The expected useful life of the listed items is based on a determination made during November, YR-2.

ITEM	EXPECTED USEFUL LIFE	REPLACEMENT COSTS
1. Roof	20–40 years	810,000
2. Awnings	8 years	7,500
3. Asphalt Paving	20 years	20,000
4. Fire Pump	40 years	8,500
5. Jockey Pump	10 years	500
6. Elevator	30 years	51,000
7. Carpet in Public Areas	5–8 years	9,000
8. Gutters & Downspouts	12 years	70,000
9. Project Security System	8–9 years	3,000
10. Entry Gate Motor	20 years	3,000
11. Pool Deck Tile	20 years	6,000
12. Pool Filter Equipment	10 years	2,000
13. Pool Electrical	10 years	1,000
14. Wood Fencing	15 years	5,000
15. Heat Pump, Pool Bldg.	10 years	6,000
16. Corr. Elec. Baseboard Heat	15 years	3,000
17. Toilet Fixtures, Pool Bldg.	20 years	3,000
18. Sauna, Pool Bldg.	20 years	5,000
19. Kitchen Appliances, Pool Bldg.	10 years	2,500
		287,000

Note 1: The above cost information was obtained from *Means Cost Guide*, YR-2, and from Li Builders.

Several common elements were not listed above because they have no expected useful life as defined in the Nita Real Estate Commission's Condominium Regulations. With normal, regular maintenance, these items should not become incapable of performing their intended function and therefore should not have to be replaced. These items are as follows:

1. **Concrete Walks, Curbs**: This assumes regular annual patching and occasional replacing of segments of the walks and curbs, as well as other maintenance.

2. **Pool Shell**: This assumes regular resurfacing and repainting of the pool shell as well as other maintenance. Such maintenance may be expected to run $3,000 annually.

3. **Common Electrical System** (Service to Units): Assuming that the system was properly installed initially (and this is in no way guaranteed by our inspection), the copper wiring and main service panels and disconnects should not need total replacement for the life of the structure. This does not preclude the possibility of the system becoming outdated or the need for ongoing maintenance. Some periodic replacement of individual outlets, fixtures, and other equipment will over time be necessary. This work has been considered part of normal maintenance.

4. **Common Plumbing System** (Plumbing to Units): The entire plumbing system is new, including the connection to the city line. Assuming that the system has been properly installed, it should not require total replacement for the life of the structure. Any cast-iron piping, such as floor drains, sewer lines, and vents may wear out, but at unpredictable life spans. Some items such as plumbing fixtures, valves, and faucets will need occasional replacement, but this replacement falls more under the category of normal maintenance.

5. **Building Superstructure**: The existing building foundations, floor slabs, floor systems, roof system, exterior masonry walls, and other components of the superstructure have in many cases already had a functional useful life of over 100 years. With the minor repairs undertaken in the current renovation, as well as with normal maintenance, these items should not need replacement for the useful life of the structure. Such maintenance should include repointing of masonry joints with new mortar and replacing any wood members that are damaged in the future due to rot, moisture, or insects.

The estimated replacement cost of these items is listed below:

Estimated Replacement Cost

1.	Concrete walks, curbs	$ 85,000.00
2.	Pool shell	$ 60,000.00
3.	Common Electrical System	$ 240,000.00
4.	Common Plumbing System	$ 240,000.00
5.	Building Superstructure	$10,400,000.00
		$11,025,000.00

Note: The estimated replacement costs are based on data from *Mean's Cost Guide*, YR-2. The estimates for the common electrical, plumbing and superstructure are based on assumptions as to exact quantities of materials. The superstructure, for example, has existing material up to 100 years old for which there is no accurate way of estimating replacement value.

EXPECTED USEFUL LIFE OF MAJOR MECHANICAL COMPONENTS OF UNITS

ITEM	EXPECTED USEFUL LIFE	REPLACEMENT COSTS
1. Hot Water Heaters	10 years	$ 800 each
2. Heat Pumps	10 years	$10,000 each
3. Whirlpool	20 years	$ 9,000 each
4. Sauna	20 years	$12,000 each
		$31,800 each

Note 1: The above cost information was obtained from *Means Cost Guide*, YR-2, and from Li Builders.

DEFENDANTS' EXHIBITS

DEFENDANT'S EXHIBITS

Defendants' Exhibit 1

THE AMERICAN INSTITUTE OF ARCHITECTS

AIA Document A201

General Conditions of the Contract for Construction

THIS DOCUMENT HAS IMPORTANT LEGAL CONSEQUENCES: CONSULTATION WITH AN ATTORNEY IS ENCOURAGED WITH RESPECT TO ITS MODIFICATION

20__ EDITION

TABLE OF ARTICLES

This document has been approved and endorsed by The Associated General Contractors of America.

AIA DOCUMENT A201 • GENERAL CONDITIONS OF THE CONTRACT FOR CONSTRUCTION • THIRTEENTH EDITION • AUGUST 1976

INDEX

GENERAL CONDITIONS OF THE CONTRACT FOR CONSTRUCTION

ARTICLE 1

CONTRACT DOCUMENTS

1.1 DEFINITIONS

1.1.1 THE CONTRACT DOCUMENTS

The Contract Documents consist of the Owner-Contractor Agreement, the Conditions of the Contract (General, Supplementary and other Conditions)), the Drawings, the Specifications, and all Addenda issued prior to and all Modifications issued after execution of the Contract. A Modification is (1) a written amendment to the Contract signed by both parties, (2) a Change Order, (3) a written interpretation issued by the Architect pursuant to Subparagraph 2.2.8, or (4) a written order for a minor change in the Work issued by the Architect pursuant to Paragraph 12.4. The Contract Documents do not include Bidding Documents such as the Advertisement of Invitation to Bid, the Instructions to Bidders, sample forms, the Contractor's Bid or portions of Addenda relating to any of these, or any other documents, unless specifically enumerated in the Owner-Contractor Agreement.

1.1.2 THE CONTRACT

The Contract Documents form the Contract for Construction. This Contract represents the entire and integrated agreement between the parties hereto and supersedes all prior negotiations, representations, or agreements, either written or oral. The Contract may be amended or modified only by a Modification as defined in Subparagraph 1.1.1. The Contract Documents shall not be construed to create any contractual relationship of any kind between the Architect and the Contractor, but the Architect shall be entitled to performance of obligations intended for his benefit, and to enforcement thereof. Nothing contained in the Contract Documents shall create any contractual relationship between the Owner or the Architect and any Subcontractor or Sub-subcontractor.

1.1.3 THE WORK

The Work comprises the completed construction required by the Contract Documents and includes all labor necessary to produce such construction, and all materials and equipment incorporated or to be incorporated in such construction.

1.1.4 THE PROJECT

The Project is the total construction of which the Work performed under the Contract Documents may be the whole or a part.

1.2 EXECUTION, CORRELATION AND INTENT

1.2.1 The Contract Documents shall be signed in not less than triplicate by the Owner and Contractor. If either the Owner or the Contractor or both do not sign the Conditions of the Contract, Drawings, Specifications, or any of the other Contract Documents, the Architect shall identify such Documents.

1.2.2 By executing the Contract, the Contractor represents that he has visited the site, familiarized himself with the local conditions under which the Work is to be performed, and correlated his observations with the requirements of the Contract Documents.

1.2.3 The intent of the Contract Documents is to include all items necessary for the proper execution and completion of the Work, The Contract Documents are complementary, and what is required by any one shall be as binding as if required by all. Work not covered in the Contract Documents will not be required unless it is consistent therewith and is reasonably inferable therefrom as being necessary to produce the intended results. Words and abbreviations which have well-known technical or trade meanings are used in the Contract Documents in accordance with such recognized meanings.

1.2.4 The organization of the Specifications into divisions, sections and articles, and the arrangement of Drawings shall not control the Contractor in dividing the Work among Subcontractors or in establishing the extent of Work to be performed by any trade.

1.3 OWNERSHIP AND USE OF DOCUMENTS

1.3.1 All Drawings, Specifications and copies thereof furnished by the Architect are and shall remain the property owner. They are to be used only with respect to this Project and are not to be used on any other project. With the exception of one contract set for each party to the Contract, such documents are to be returned or suitably accounted for to the owner on request at the completion of the Work. ~~Submission or distribution to meet official regulatory requirements or for other purposes in connection with the Project is not to be construed as publication in derogation of the Architect's common law copyright or other reserved rights.~~

ARTICLE 2

ARCHITECT

2.1 DEFINITION

2.1.1 The Architect is the person lawfully licensed to practice architecture, or an entity lawfully practicing architecture identified as such in the Owner-Contractor Agreement, and is referred to throughout the Contract Documents as if singular in number and masculine in gender. The term Architect means the Architect or his authorized representative.

2.2 ADMINISTRATION OF THE CONTRACT

2.2.1 The Architect will provide administration of the Contract as hereinafter described.

2.2.2 The Architect will be the Owner's representative during construction and until final payment is due. The Architect will advise and consult with the Owner. The Owner's instructions to the Contractor shall be forwarded through the Architect. The Architect will have authority to act on behalf of the Owner only to

the extent provided in the Contract Documents, unless otherwise modified by written instrument in accordance with Subparagraph 2.2.18.

2.2.3 The Architect will visit the site at intervals appropriate to the stage of construction to familiarize himself generally with the progress and quality of the Work and to determine in general if the Work is proceeding in accordance with the Contract Documents. ~~However, the Architect will not be required to make exhaustive or continuous on-site inspections to check the quality or quantity of the Work.~~ On the basis of his on-site observations as an architect, he will keep the Owner informed of the progress of the Work, and will endeavor to guard the Owner against defects and deficiencies in the Work of the Contractor.

2.2.4 The Architect will not be responsible for and will not have control or charge of construction means, methods, techniques, sequences or procedures, or for safety precautions and programs in connection with the Work, and he will not be responsible for the Contractor's failure to carry out the Work in accordance with the Contract Documents. The Architect will not be responsible for or have control or charge over the acts or omissions of the Contractor, Subcontractors, or any of their agents or employee, or any other persons performing any of the Work other than as set forth herein.

2.2.5 The Architect shall at all times have access to the Work wherever it is in preparation and progress. The Contractor shall provide facilities for such access so the Architect may perform his functions under the Contract Documents.

2.2.6 Based on the Architect's observations and an evaluation of the Contractor's Applications for Payment, the Architect will determine the amounts owing to the Contractor and will issue Certificates for Payment in such amounts, as provided in Paragraph 9.4.

2.2.7 The Architect will be the interpreter of the requirements of the Contract Documents and the judge of the performance thereunder by both the Owner and Contractor.

2.2.8   The Architect will render interpretations necessary for the proper execution or progress of the Work, with reasonable promptness and in accordance with any time limit agreed upon. Either party to the Contract may make written request to the Architect for such interpretations.

2.2.9   Claims, disputes and other matters in question between the Contractor and the Owner relating to the execution or progress of the Work or the interpretation of the Contract Documents shall be referred initially to the Architect for decision which he will render in writing with a reasonable time.

2.2.10 All interpretations and decisions of the Architect shall be consistent with the intent of and reasonably inferable from the Contract Documents and will be in writing or in the form of drawings. In his capacity as interpreter and judge, he will endeavor to secure faithful performance by both the Owner and the Contractor, will not show partiality to either, and will not be liable for the result of any interpretation or decision rendered in good faith in such capacity, consistent with his responsibilities herein.

2.2.11 The Architect's decisions in matters relating to artistic effect will be final if consistent with the intent of the Contract Documents.

2.2.12 Any claim, dispute or other matter in question between the Contractor and the Owner referred to the Architect, except those relating to artistic effect as provided in Subparagraph 2.2.11 and except those which have been waived by the making or acceptance of final payment as provided in Subparagraphs 9.9.4 and 9.9.5, shall be subject to arbitration upon the written demand of either party. However, no demand for arbitration of any such claim, dispute or other matter may be made until the earlier of (1) the date on which the Architect has rendered a written decision, or (2) the tenth day after the parties have presented their evidence to the Architect or have been given a reasonable opportunity to do so, if the Architect has not rendered his written decision by that date. When such a written decision of the Architect states (1) that the decision is final bus subject to appeal, and (2) that

any demand for arbitration of a claim, dispute or other matter covered by such a decision must be made within thirty days after the date on which the party making the demand receives the written decision, failure to demand arbitration within said thirty days' period will result in the Architect's decision becoming final and binding upon the Owner and the Contractor. If the Architect renders a decision after arbitration proceedings have been initiated, such decision may be entered as evidence but will not supersede any arbitration proceedings unless the decision is acceptable to all parties concerned.

2.2.13 The Architect will have authority to reject Work which does not conform to the Contract Documents. Whenever, in his opinion, he considers it necessary or advisable for the implementation of the intent of the Contract Documents, he will have authority to require special inspection or testing of the Work in accordance with Subparagraph 7.7.2 whether or not such Work be then fabricated, installed or completed. However, neither the Architect's authority to act under this Subparagraph 2.2.13, nor any decision made by him in good faith either to exercise or not to exercise such authority, shall give rise to any duty or responsibility of the Architect to the Contractor, any Subcontractor, any of their agents or employees, or any other person performing any of the Work consistent with his responsibilities herein.

2.2.14 The Architect will review and approve or take other appropriate action upon Contractor's submittals such as Shop Drawings, Product Data and Samples, but only for conformance with the design concept of the Work and with the information given in the Contract Documents. Such action shall be taken with reasonable promptness so as to cause no delay. The Architect's approval of a specific item shall no indicate approval of an assembly of which the item is a component.

2.2.15 The Architect will prepare Change Orders in accordance with Article 12, and will have authority to order minor changes in the Work as provided in Subparagraph 12.4.1.

2.2.16 The Architect will conduct inspections to determine the dates of Substantial Completion and final completion, will receive and forward to the Owner for the Owner's review written warranties and related documents required by the Contract and assembled by the Contractor, and will issue a final Certificate for Payment upon compliance with the requirements of Paragraph 9.9.

2.2.17 If the Owner and Architect agree, the Architect will provide one or more Project Representatives to assist the Architect in carrying out his responsibilities at the site. The duties, responsibilities and limitations of authority of any such Project Representative shall be as set forth in an exhibit to be incorporated in the Contract Documents.

2.2.18 The duties, responsibilities and limitations of authority of the Architect as the Owner's representative during construction as set forth in the Contract Documents will not be modified or extended without written consent of the Owner, the Contractor and the Architect.

2.2.19 In case of the termination of the employment of the Architect, the Owner shall appoint an architect against whom the Contractor makes no reasonable objection whose status under the Contract Documents shall be that of the former architect. Any dispute in connection with such appointment shall be subject to arbitration.

ARTICLE 3

OWNER

3.1 DEFINITION

3.1 The Owner is the person or entity identified as such in the Owner-Contractor Agreement and is referred to throughout the Contract Documents as if singular in number and masculine in gender. The term Owner means the Owner or his authorized representative.

3.2 INFORMATION AND SERVICES REQUIRED OF THE OWNER

3.2.1 The Owner shall, at the request of the Contractor at the time of execution of the Owner Contractor Agreement, furnish to the Contractor reasonable evidence that he has made financial arrangements to fulfill his obligations under the Contract, Unless such reasonable evidence is furnished, the Contractor is not required to execute the Owner-Contractor Agreement or to commence the Work.

3.2.2. The Owner shall furnish all surveys describing the physical characteristics, legal limitations and utility locations for the site of the Project, and a legal description of the site.

3.2.3 Except as provided in Subparagraph 4.7.1, the Owner shall secure and pay for necessary approvals, easements, assessments and charges required for the construction, use or occupancy of permanent structures or for permanent changes in existing facilities.

3.2.4 Information or services under the Owner's control shall be furnished by the Owner with reasonable promptness to avoid delay in the orderly progress of the Work.

3.2.5 Unless otherwise provided in the Contract Documents, the Contractor will be furnished, free of charge, all copies of Drawings and Specifications reasonably necessary for the execution of the Work.

3.2.6 The Owner shall forward all instructions to the Contractor through the Architect

3.2.7 The foregoing are in addition to other duties and responsibilities of the Owner enumerated herein and especially those in respect to Work by Owner or by Separate Contractors, Payments and Completion, and insurance in Articles 6, 9 and 11 respectively.

3.3 OWNER'S RIGHT TO STOP THE WORK

3.3.1 If the Contractor fails to correct defective Work as required by Paragraph 13.2 or persistently fails to carry out the Work in accordance with the Contract Documents, the Owner, by a written order signed personally or by an agent specifically so empowered by the Owner in writing, may order the Contractor to stop the Work, or any portion thereof, until the cause for such order has been eliminated; however, this right of the Owner to stop the Work shall not give rise to any duty on the part of the Owner to exercise this right for the benefit of the Contractor or any other person or entity, except to the extent required by Subparagraph 6.1.3.

3.4 OWNER'S RIGHT TO CARRY OUT THE WORK

3.4.1 If the Contractor defaults or neglects to carry out the Work in accordance with the Contract Documents and fails within seven days after receipt of written notice from the Owner to commence and continue correction of such default or neglect with diligence and promptness, the Owner may, after seven days following receipt by the Contractor of an additional written notice and without prejudice to any other remedy he may have, make good such deficiencies. In such case an appropriate Change Order shall be issued deducting from the payments then or thereafter due the Contractor the cost of correcting such deficiencies, including compensation for the Architect's additional services made necessary by such default, neglect or failure. Such action by the Owner and the amount charged to the Contractor are both subject to the prior approval of the Architect. If the payments then or thereafter due the Contractor are not sufficient to cover such amount, the Contractor shall pay the difference to the Owner.

ARTICLE 4

CONTRACTOR

4.1. DEFINITION

4.1.1 The Contractor is the person or entity identified as such in the Owner-Contractor Agreement and is referred to throughout the Contract Documents as if singular in number and masculine in gender. The term Contractor means the Contractor or his authorized representative.

4.2 REVIEW OF CONTRACT DOCUMENTS

4.2.1 The Contractor shall carefully study and compare the Contract Documents and shall at once report to the Architect any error,

inconsistency or omission he may discover. The Contractor shall not be liable to the Owner or the Architect for any damage resulting from any such errors, inconsistencies or omissions in the Contract Documents. The Contractor shall perform no portion of the Work at any time without Contract Documents or, where required, approved Shop Drawings, Product Data or Samples for such portion of the Work.

4.3 SUPERVISION AND CONSTRUCTION PROCEDURES

4.3.1 The Contractor shall supervise and direct the Work, using his best skill and attention. He shall be solely responsible for all construction means, methods, techniques, sequences and procedures and for coordinating all portions of the Work under the Contract.

4.3.2 The Contractor shall be responsible to the Owner for the acts and omissions of his employees, Subcontractors and their agents and employees, and other persons performing any of the Work under a contract with the Contractor.

4.3.3 The Contractor shall not be relieved from his obligations to perform the Work in accordance with the Contract Documents either by the activities or duties of the Architect in his administration of the Contract, or by inspections, tests or approvals required or performed under Paragraph 7.7 by persons other than the Contractor.

4.4 LABOR AND MATERIALS

4.4.1 Unless otherwise provided in the Contract Documents, the Contractor shall provide and pay for all labor, materials, equipment, tools, construction equipment and machinery, water, heat, utilities, transportation, and other facilities and services necessary for the proper execution and completion of the Work, whether temporary or permanent and whether or not incorporated or to be incorporated in the Work.

4.4.2 The Contractor shall at all times enforce strict discipline and good order among his employees and shall not employ on the Work any unfit person or anyone not skilled in the task assigned to him.

4.5 WARRANTY

4.5.1 The Contractor warrants to the Owner and the Architect that all materials and equipment furnished under this Contract will be new unless otherwise specified, and that all Work will be of good quality, free from faults and defects and in conformance with the Contract Documents. All Work not conforming to these requirements, including substitutions not properly approved and authorized, may be considered defective. If required by the Architect, the Contractor shall furnish satisfactory evidence as to the kind and quality of materials and equipment. This warranty is not limited by the provisions of Paragraph 13.2.

4.6 TAXES

4.6.1 The Contractor shall pay all sales, consumer, use and other similar taxes for the Work or portions thereof provided by the Contractor which are legally enacted at the time bids are received, whether or not yet effective.

4.7 PERMITS, FEES AND NOTICES

4.7.1 Unless otherwise provided in the Contract Documents, the Contractor shall secure and pay for the building permit and for all other permits and governmental fees, licenses and inspections necessary for the proper execution and completion of the Work which are customarily secured after execution of the Contract and which are legally required at the time the bids are received, including an occupancy certificate or permit.

4.7.2 The Contractor shall give all notices and comply with all laws, ordinances, rules, regulations and lawful orders of any public authority bearing on the performance of the Work.

4.7.3 It is not the responsibility of the Contractor to make certain that the Contract Documents are in accordance with applicable laws, statutes, building codes and regulations. If the Contractor observes that any of the Contract Documents are at variance therewith in any respect, he shall promptly notify the Architect in writing, and

any necessary changes shall be accomplished by appropriate Modification.

4.7.4 If the Contractor performs any Work knowing it to be contrary to such laws, ordinances, rules and regulations, and without such notice to the Architect, he shall assume full responsibility therefor and shall bear all costs attributable thereto.

4.8 ALLOWANCES

4.8.1 The Contractor shall include in the Contract Sum all allowances stated in the Contract Documents. Items covered by these allowances shall be supplied for such amounts and by such persons as the Owner may direct, but the Contractor will not be required to employ persons against whom he makes a reasonable objection.

4.8.2 Unless otherwise provided in the Contract Documents:

1. these allowances shall cover the cost to the Contractor, less any applicable trade discount, of the materials and equipment required by the allowance delivered at the site, and all applicable taxes;

2. the Contractor's costs for unloading and handling on the site, labor, installation costs, overhead, profit and other expenses contemplated for the original allowance shall be included in the Contract Sum and not in the allowance;

3. whenever the cost is more than or less than the allowance, the Contract Sum shall be adjusted accordingly by Change Order, the amount of which will recognize changes, if any, in handling costs on the site, labor, installation costs, overhead, profit and other expenses.

4.9 SUPERINTENDENT

4.9.1 The Contractor shall employ a competent superintendent who shall represent the Contractor and all communications given to the superintendent shall be as binding as if given to the Contractor. Important communications shall be so confirmed on written request in each case.

4.10 PROGRESS SCHEDULE

4.10.1 The Contractor, immediately after being awarded the Contract, shall prepare and submit for the Owner's and Architect's information an estimated progress schedule for the Work. The progress schedule shall be related to the entire Project to the extent required by the Contract Documents, and shall provide for expeditious and practicable execution of the Work.

4.11 DOCUMENTS AND SAMPLES AT THE SITE

4.11.1 The Contractor shall maintain at the site for the Owner one record copy of all Drawings, Specifications, Addenda, Change Orders and other Modifications, in good order and marked currently to record all changes made during construction, and approved Shop Drawings, Product Data and Samples. These shall be available to the Architect and shall be delivered to him for the Owner upon completion of the Work.

4.12 SHOP DRAWINGS, PRODUCT DATA AND SAMPLES

4.12.1 Shop Drawings are drawings, diagrams, schedules and other data specially prepared for the Work by the Contractor or any Subcontractor, manufacturer, supplier or distributor to illustrate some portion of the Work.

4.12.2 Samples are physical examples which illustrate materials, equipment or workmanship and establish standards by which the Work will be judged.

4.12.3 The Contractor shall review, approve and submit, with reasonable promptness and in such sequence as to cause no delay in the Work or in the work of the Owner or any separate contractor, all Shop Drawings, Product Data and Samples required by the Contract Documents.

4.12.4 By approving and submitting Shop Drawings, Product Data and Samples, the Contractor represents that he has determined and verified all materials, field measurements, and field construction criteria related thereto, or will do so, and that he has checked and coordinated the information contained with such submittals

with the requirements of the Work and of the Contract Documents.

4.12.5 The Contractor shall not be relieved of responsibility for any deviation from the requirements of the Contract Documents by the Architect's approval of Shop Drawings, Product Data or Samples under Subparagraph 2.2.14 unless the Contractor has specifically informed the Architect in writing of such deviation at the time of submission and the Architect has given written approval to the specific deviation. The Contractor shall not be relieved from responsibility for errors or omissions in the Shop Drawings, Product Data or Samples by the Architect's approval thereof.

4.12.6 The Contractor shall direct specific attention, in writing or on resubmitted Shop Drawings, Product Data or Samples, to revisions other than those requested by the Architect on previous submittals.

4.12.7 No portion of the Work requiring submission of a Shop Drawing, Product Data or Sample shall be commenced until the submittal has been approved by the Architect as provided in Subparagraph 2.2.14. All such portions of the Work shall be in accordance with approved submittals.

4.13 USE OF SITE

4.13.1 The Contractor shall confine operations at the site to areas permitted by law, ordinances, permits and the Contract Documents and shall no unreasonably encumber the site with any materials or equipment.

4.14 CUTTING AND PATCHING OF WORK

4.14.1 The Contractor shall be responsible for all cutting, fitting or patching that may be required to complete the Work or to make its several parts fit together properly.

4.14.2 The Contractor shall not damage or endanger any portion of the Work or the work of the Owner or any separate contractors by cutting, patching, or otherwise altering any work, or by excavation. The Contractor shall not cut or otherwise alter the work of the Owner or any separate contractor except with the written consent of the Owner and of such separate contractor. The Contractor shall not unreasonably withhold from the Owner or any separate contractor his consent to cutting or otherwise altering the Work.

4.15   CLEANING UP

4.15.1 The Contractor at all times shall keep the premises free from accumulation of waste materials or rubbish caused by his operations. At the completion of the Work he shall remove all his waste materials and rubbish from and about the Project as well as all his tools, construction equipment, machinery and surplus materials.

4.15.2 If the Contractor fails to clean up at the completion of the Work, the Owner may do so as provided in Paragraph 3.4 and the cost thereof shall be charged to the Contractor.

4.16   COMMUNICATIONS

4.16.1 The Contractor shall forward all communications to the Owner through the Architect

4.17   ROYALTIES AND PATENTS

4.17.1 The Contractor shall pay all royalties and license fees. He shall defend all suits or claims for infringement of any patent rights and shall save the Owner harmless from loss on account thereof, except that the Owner shall be responsible for all such loss when a particular design, process or the product of a particular manufacturer or manufacturers is specified, but if the Contractor has reason to believe that the design, process or product specified is an infringement of a patent, he shall be responsible for such loss unless he promptly gives such information to the Architect.

4.18   INDEMNIFICATION

4.18.1 To the fullest extent permitted by law, the Contractor shall indemnify and hold harmless the Owner and the Architect and their agents and employees from and against all claims, damages, losses and expenses, including but not limited to attorney's fees, arising out of or resulting from the performance of the Work, provided

that any such claim, damage, loss or expense (1) is attributable to bodily injury, sickness, disease or death, or to injury to or destruction of tangible property (other than the Work itself) including the loss of use resulting therefrom, and (2) is caused in whole or in part by any negligent act or omission of the Contractor, any Subcontractor, anyone directly or indirectly employed by any of them or anyone for whose acts any of them may be liable, regardless of whether or not it is caused in part by a party indemnified hereunder. Such obligation shall not be construed to negate, abridge, or otherwise reduce any other right or obligation of indemnity which would otherwise exist as to any party or person described in this Paragraph 4.18.

4.18.2 In any and all claims against the Owner or the Architect or any of their agents or employees by any employee of the Contractor, any Subcontractor, anyone directly or indirectly employed by any of them or anyone for whose acts any of them may be liable, the indemnification obligation under this Paragraph 4.18 shall not be limited in any way by any limitation on the amount or type of damages, compensation or benefits payable by or for the Contractor or any Subcontractor under workers' or workmen's compensation acts, disability benefit acts or other employee benefit acts.

4.18.3 The obligations of the Contractor under this Paragraph 4.18 shall not extend to the liability of the Architect, his agents or employees, arising out of (1) the preparation or approval of maps, drawings, opinions, reports, surveys, change orders, designs or specifications, or (2) the giving of or the failure to give directions or instructions by the Architect, his agents or employees provided such giving or failure to give is the primary cause of the injury or damage.

ARTICLE 5

SUBCONTRACTORS

5.1   DEFINITION

5.1.1   A Subcontractor is a person or entity who has a direct contract with the Contractor to perform any of the Work at the site. The term Subcontractor is referred to throughout the Contract Documents as if singular in number and masculine in gender and means a Subcontractor or his authorized representative. The term Subcontractor does not include any separate contractor or his subcontractors.

5.1.2 A Sub-subcontractor is a person or entity who has a direct or indirect contract with a Subcontractor to perform any of the Work at the site. The term Sub-subcontractor is referred to throughout the Contract Documents as if singular in number and masculine in gender and means a Sub-subcontractor or an authorized representative thereof.

5.2 AWARD OF SUBCONTRACTS AND OTHER CONTRACTS FOR PORTIONS OF THE WORK

5.2.1 Unless otherwise required by the Contract Documents or the Bidding Documents, the Contractor, as soon as practicable after the award of the Contract, shall furnish to the Owner and the Architect in writing the names of the persons or entities (including those who are to furnish materials or equipment fabricated to a special design) proposed for each of the principal portions of the Work. The Architect will promptly reply to the Contractor in writing stating whether or not the Owner or the Architect, after due investigation, has reasonable objection to any such proposed person or entity. Failure of the Owner or Architect to reply promptly shall constitute notice of no reasonable objection.

5.2.2 The Contractor shall not contract with any such proposed person or entity to whom the Owner or the Architect has made reasonable objection under the provisions of Subparagraph 5.2.1. The Contractor shall not be required to contract with anyone to whom he has a reasonable objection.

5.2.3 If the Owner or the Architect has reasonable objection to any such proposed person or entity, the Contractor shall submit a substitute to whom the Owner or the Architect has no reasonable objection, and the Contract Sum

shall be increased or decreased by the difference in cost occasioned by such substitution and an appropriate Change Order shall be issued; however, no increase in the Contract Sum shall be allowed for any such substitution unless the Contractor has acted promptly and responsively in submitting names as required by Subparagraph 5.2.1.

5.2.4. The Contractor shall make no substitution for any Subcontractor, person or entity previously selected if the Owner or Architect makes reasonable objection to such substitution.

5.3 SUBCONTRACTUAL RELATIONS

5.3.1 By an appropriate agreement, written where legally required for validity, the Contractor shall require each Subcontractor, to the extent of the Work to be performed by the Subcontractor, to be bound to the Contractor by the terms of the Contract Documents, and to assume toward the Contractor all the obligations and responsibilities which the Contractor, by these Documents, assumes toward the Owner and the Architect. Said agreement shall preserve and protect the rights of the Owner and the Architect under the Contract Documents with respect to the Work to be performed by the Subcontractor so that the subcontracting thereof will not prejudice such rights, and shall allow to the Subcontractor, unless specifically provided otherwise in the Contractor-Subcontractor agreement, the benefit of all rights, remedies and redress against the Contractor that the Contractor, by these Documents, has against the Owner. Where appropriate, the Contractor shall require each Subcontractor to enter into similar agreements with his Sub-subcontractors. The Contractor shall make available to each proposed Subcontractor, prior to the execution of the Subcontract, copies of the Contract Documents to which the Subcontractor will be bound by this Paragraph 5.3, and identify to the Subcontractor any terms and conditions of the proposed Subcontract which may be at variance with the Contract Documents. Each Subcontractor shall similarly make copies of such Documents available to his Sub-subcontractors.

ARTICLE 6

WORK BY OWNER OR BY SEPARATE CONTRACTORS

6.1 OWNER'S RIGHT TO PERFORM WORK AND TO AWARD SEPARATE CONTRACTS

6.1.1 The Owner reserves the right to perform work related to the Project with his own forces, and to award separate contracts in connection with other portions of the Project or other work on the site under these or similar Conditions of the Contract. If the Contractor claims that delay or additional cost is involved because of such action by the Owner, he shall make such claim as provided elsewhere in the Contract Documents.

6.1.2 When separate contracts are awarded for different portions of the Project or other work on the site, the term Contractor in the Contract Documents in each case shall mean the Contractor who executes each separate Owner-Contractor Agreement.

6.1.3 The Owner will provide for the coordination of the work of his own forces and of each separate contractor with the Work of the Contractor, who shall cooperate therewith as provided in Paragraph 6.2.

6.2 MUTUAL RESPONSIBILITY

6.2.1 The Contractor shall afford the Owner and separate contractors reasonable opportunity for the introduction and storage of their materials and equipment and the execution of their work, and shall connect and coordinate his Work with theirs as required by the Contract Documents.

6.2.2 If any part of the Contractor's Work depends for proper execution or results upon the work of the Owner or any separate contractor, the Contractor shall, prior to proceeding with the Work, promptly report to the Architect any apparent discrepancies or defects in such other work that render it unsuitable for such proper execution and results. Failure of the Contractor

so to report shall constitute an acceptance of the Owner's or separate contractors' work as fit and proper to receive his Work, except as to defects which may subsequently become apparent in such work by others.

6.2.3 Any costs caused by defective or ill-timed work shall be borne by the party responsible therefor.

6.2.4 Should the Contractor wrongfully cause damage to the work or property of the Owner, or to other work on the site, the Contractor shall promptly remedy such damage as provided in Subparagraph 10.2.5.

6.2.5 Should the Contractor wrongfully cause damage to the work or property of any separate contractor, the Contractor shall upon due notice promptly attempt to settle with such other contractor by agreement, or otherwise to resolve the dispute. If such separate contractor sues or initiates an arbitration proceeding against the Owner on account of any damage alleged to have been caused by the Contractor, the Owner shall notify the Contractor who shall defend such proceedings at the Owner's expense, and if any judgment or award against the Owner arises therefrom the Contractor shall pay or satisfy it and shall reimburse the Owner for all attorneys' fees and court or arbitration costs which the Owner has incurred.

6.3 OWNER'S RIGHT TO CLEAN UP

6.3.1 If a dispute arises between the Contractor and separate contractors as to their responsibility for cleaning up as required by Paragraph 4.15 the Owner may clean up and charge the cost thereof to the contractors responsible therefor as the Architect shall determine to be just.

ARTICLE 7

MISCELLANEOUS PROVISIONS

7.1 GOVERNING LAW

7.1.1 The Contract shall be governed by the law of the place where the Project is located.

7.2 SUCCESSORS AND ASSIGNS

7.2.1 The Owner and the Contractor each binds himself, his partners, successors, assigns and legal representatives to the other party hereto and to the partners, successors, assigns and legal representatives of such other party with respect to all covenants, agreements and obligations contained in the Contract Documents. Neither party to the Contract shall assign the Contract or sublet it as a whole without the written consent of the other, nor shall the Contractor assign any moneys due or to become due to him hereunder, without the previous written consent of the Owner.

7.3 WRITTEN NOTICE

7.3.1 Written notice shall be deemed to have been duly served if delivered in person to the individual or member of the firm or entity or to an officer of the corporation for whom it was intended, or if delivered at or sent by registered or certified mail to the last business address known to him who gives the notice.

7.4 CLAIMS FOR DAMAGES

7.4.1 Should either party to the Contract suffer injury or damage to person or property because of any act or omission of the other party or of any of his employees, agents or others for whose acts he is legally liable, claim shall be made in writing to such other party within a reasonable time after the first observance of such injury or damage.

7.5 PERFORMANCE BOND AND LABOR AND MATERIAL PAYMENT BOND

7.5.1 The Owner shall have the right to require the Contractor to furnish bonds covering the faithful performance of the Contract and the payment of all obligations arising thereunder if and as required in the Bidding Documents or in the Contract Documents.

7.6 RIGHTS AND REMEDIES

7.6.1 The duties and obligations imposed by the Contract Documents and the rights and remedies available thereunder shall be in addition to and not a limitation of any duties, obligations, rights and remedies otherwise imposed or available by law.

7.6.2 No action or failure to act by the Owner, Architect or Contractor shall constitute a waiver of any right or duty afforded any of them under the Contract, nor shall any such action or failure to act constitute an approval of or acquiescence in any breach thereunder, except as may be specifically agreed in writing.

7.7 TESTS

7.7.1 If the Contract Documents, laws, ordinances, rules, regulations or orders of any public authority having jurisdiction require any portion of the Work to be inspected, tested or approved, the Contractor shall give the Architect timely notice of its readiness so the Architect may observe such inspection, testing or approval. The Contractor shall bear all costs of such inspections, tests, or approvals conducted by public authorities. Unless otherwise provided, the Owner shall bear all costs of other inspections, tests or approvals.

7.7.2 If the Architect determines that any Work requires special inspection, testing, or approval which Subparagraph 7.7.1 does not include, he will, upon written authorization from the Owner, instruct the Contractor to order such special inspection, testing or approval, and the Contractor shall give notice as provided in Subparagraph 7.7.1. If such special inspection or testing reveals a failure of the Work to comply with the requirements of the Contract Documents, the Contractor shall bear all costs thereof, including compensation for the Architect's additional services made necessary by such failure; otherwise the Owner shall bear such costs, and an appropriate Change Order shall be issued.

7.7.3 Required certificates of inspection, testing or approval shall be secured by the Contractor and promptly delivered by him to the Architect.

7.7.4 If the Architect is to observe the inspections, tests or approvals required by the Contract

Documents, he will do so promptly and, where practicable, at the source of supply.

7.8 INTEREST

7.8.1 Payments due and unpaid under the Contract Documents shall bear interest from the date payment is due at such rate as the parties may agree upon in writing or, in the absence thereof, at the legal rate prevailing at the place of the Project.

7.9 ARBITRATION

7.9.1 All claims, disputes and other matters in question between the Contractor and the Owner arising out of, or relating to, the Contract Documents or the breach thereof, except as provided in Subparagraph 2.2.11 with respect to the Architect's decisions on matters relating to artistic effect, and except for claims which have been waived by the making or acceptance of final payment as provided by Subparagraphs 9.9.4 and 9.9.5, shall be decided by arbitration in accordance with the Construction Industry Arbitration Rules of the American Arbitration Association then obtaining unless the parties mutually agree otherwise. No arbitration arising out of or relating to the Contract Documents shall include, by consolidation, joinder or in any other manner, the Architect, his employees or consultants except by written consent containing a specific reference to the Owner-Contractor Agreement and signed by the Architect, the Owner, the Contractor and any other person sought to be joined. No arbitration shall include by consolidation, joinder or in any other manner, parties other than the Owner, the Contractor and any other per- sons substantially involved in a common question of fact or law, whose presence is required if complete relief is to be accorded in the arbitration. No person other than the Owner or Contractor shall be included as an original third party or additional third party to an arbitration whose interest or responsibility is insubstantial. Any consent to arbitration involving an additional person or persons shall not constitute consent to arbitration of any dispute not described therein or with any person not named or described therein. The foregoing agreement to arbitrate and any other

agreement to arbitrate with an additional person or persons duly consented to by the parties to the Owner-Contractor Agreement shall be specifically enforceable under the prevailing arbitration law. The award rendered by the arbitrators shall be final, and judgment may be entered upon it in accordance with applicable law in any court having jurisdiction thereof.

7.9.2 Notice of the demand for arbitration shall be filed in writing with the other party to the Owner-Contractor Agreement and with the American Arbitration Association, and a copy shall be filed with the Architect. The demand for arbitration shall be made within the time limits specified in Subparagraph 2.2.12 where applicable, and in all other cases within a reasonable time after the claim, dispute or other matter in question has arisen, and in no event shall it be made after the date when institution of legal or equitable proceedings based on such claim, dispute or other matter in question would be barred by the applicable statute of limitations.

7.9.3 Unless otherwise agreed in writing, the Contractor shall carry on the Work and maintain its progress during any arbitration proceedings, and the Owner shall continue to make payments to the Contractor in accordance with the Contract Documents.

ARTICLE 8
TIME

8.1 DEFINITIONS

8.1.1 Unless otherwise provided, the Contract Time is the period of time allotted in the Contract Documents for Substantial Completion of the Work as defined in Subparagraph 8.1.3, including authorized adjustments thereto.

8.1.2 The date of commencement of the Work is the date established in a notice to proceed. If there is no notice to proceed, it shall be the date of the Owner-Contractor Agreement or such other date as may be established therein.

8.1.3 The Date of Substantial Completion of the Work or designated portion thereof is the Date certified by the Architect when construction is sufficiently complete, in accordance with the Contract Documents, so the Owner can occupy or utilize the Work or designated portion thereof for the use for which it is intended.

8.1.4   The term day as used in the Contract Documents shall mean calendar day unless otherwise specifically designated.

8.2   PROGRESS AND COMPLETION

8.2.1   All time limits stated in the Contract Documents are of the essence of the Contract.

8.2.2   The Contractor shall begin the Work on the date of commencement as defined in Subparagraph 8.1.2. He shall carry the Work forward expeditiously with adequate forces and shall achieve Substantial Completion within the Contract Time.

8.3   DELAYS AND EXTENSIONS OF TIME

8.3.1   If the Contractor is delayed at any time in the progress of the Work by any act or neglect of the Owner or the Architect, or by any employee of either, or by any separate contractor employed by the Owner, or by changes ordered in the Work, or by labor disputes, fire, unusual delay in transportation, adverse weather conditions not reasonably anticipatable, unavoidable casualties, or any causes beyond the Contractor's control, or by delay authorized by the Owner pending arbitration, or by any other cause which the Architect determines may justify the delay, then the Contract Time shall be extended by Change Order for such reasonable time as the Architect may determine.

8.3.2   Any claim for extension of time shall be made in writing to the Architect not more than twenty days after the commencement of the delay; otherwise it shall be waived. In the case of a continuing delay only one claim is necessary. The Contractor shall provide an estimate of the probable effect of such delay on the progress of the Work.

8.3.3   If no agreement is made stating the dates upon which interpretations as provided in Subparagraph 2.2.8 shall be furnished, then no claim for delay shall be allowed on account of

failure to furnish such interpretations until fifteen days after written request is made for them, and not then unless such claim is reasonable.

8.3.4   This Paragraph 8.3 does not exclude the recovery of damages for delay by either party under other provisions of the Contract Documents.

ARTICLE 9
PAYMENTS AND COMPLETION

9.1   CONTRACT SUM

9.1.1   The Contract Sum is stated in the Owner-Contractor Agreement and, including authorized adjustments thereto, is the total amount payable by the Owner to the Contractor for the performance of the Work under the Contract Documents.

9.2   SCHEDULE OF VALUES

9.2.1   Before the first Application for Payment, the Contractor shall submit to the Architect a schedule of values allocated to the various portions of the Work, prepared in such form and supported by such data to substantiate its accuracy as the Architect may require. This schedule, unless objected to by the Architect, shall be used only as a basis for the Contractor's Applications for Payment.

9.3   APPLICATIONS FOR PAYMENT

9.3.1   At least ten days before the date for each progress payment established in the Owner-Contractor Agreement, the Contractor shall submit to the Architect an itemized Application for Payment, notarized if required, supported by such data substantiating the Contractor's right to payment as the Owner or the Architect may require, and reflecting retainage, if any, as provided elsewhere in the Contract Documents.

9.3.2   ~~Unless otherwise provided in the Contract Documents, payments, will be made on account of materials or equipment not incorporated in the Work but delivered and suitably stored at the site and, if approved in advance by the Owner, payments may similarly be made for~~

~~materials or equipment suitably stored at some other location agreed upon in writing. Payments for materials or equipment stored on or off the site shall be conditioned upon submission by the Contractor of bills of sale or such other procedures satisfactory to the Owner to establish the Owner's title to such materials or equipment or otherwise protect the Owner's interest, including applicable insurance and transportation to the site for these materials and equipment stored off the site.~~

9.3.3   The Contractor warrants that title to all Work, materials and equipment covered by an Application for Payment will pass to the Owner either by incorporation in the construction or upon the receipt of payment by the Contractor, whichever occurs first, free and clear of all liens, claims, security interests or encumbrances, hereinafter referred to in this Article 9 as "liens"; and that no Work, materials or equipment covered by an Application for Payment will have been acquired by the Contractor, or by any other person performing Work at the site or furnishing materials and equipment for the Project, subject to an agreement under which an interest therein or an encumbrance therein is retained by the seller or otherwise imposed by the Contractor or such other person.

9.4   CERTIFICATES FOR PAYMENT

9.4.1   The Architect will, within seven days after the receipt of the Contractor's Application for Payment, either issue a Certificate for Payment to the Owner, with a copy to the Contractor, for such amount as the Architect determines is properly due, or notify the Contractor in writing his reasons for withholding a Certificate as provided in Subparagraph 9.6.1

9.4.2   The issuance of a Certificate for Payment will constitute a representation by the Architect to the Owner, based on his observations at the site as provided in Subparagraph 2.2.3 and the data comprising the Application for Payment, that the Work has progressed to the point indicated; that, to the best of his knowledge, information and belief, the quality of the Work is in accordance with the Contract

Documents (subject to an evaluation of the Work for conformance with the Contract Documents upon Substantial Completion, to the results of any subsequent tests required by or performed under the Contract Documents, to minor deviations from the Contract Documents correctable prior to completion, and to any specific qualifications stated in his Certificate); and that the Contractor is entitled to payment in the amount certified. However, by issuing a Certificate for Payment, the Architect shall not thereby be deemed to represent that he has ~~made exhaustive or continuous on-site inspections to check the quality or quantity of the Work or that he has reviewed the construction means, methods, techniques, sequences or procedures, or that he has~~ made any examination to ascertain how or for what purpose the Contractor has used the moneys previously paid on account of the Contract Sum.

9.5   PROGRESS PAYMENTS

9.5.1   After the Architect has issued a Certificate for Payment, the Owner shall make payment in the manner and within the time provided in the Contract Documents.

9.5.2   The Contractor shall promptly pay each Subcontractor, upon receipt of payment from the Owner, out of the amount paid to the Contractor on account of such Subcontractor's Work, the amount to which said Subcontractor is entitled, reflecting the percentage actually retained, if any, from payments to the Contractor on account of such Subcontractor's Work. The Contractor shall, by an appropriate agreement with each Subcontractor, require each Subcontractor to make payments to his Sub-subcontractors in similar manner.

9.5.3   The Architect may, on request and at his discretion, furnish to any Subcontractor, if practicable, information regarding the percentages of completion or the amounts applied for by the Contractor and the action taken thereon by the Architect on account of Work done by such Subcontractor.

9.5.4   Neither the Owner nor the Architect shall have any obligation to pay or to see to the payment of any moneys to any Subcontractor except as may otherwise be required by law.

9.5.5   No Certificate for a progress payment, nor any progress payment, nor any partial or entire use or occupancy of the Project by the Owner, shall constitute an acceptance of any Work no in accordance with the Contract Documents.

9.6   PAYMENTS WITHHELD

9.6.1   The Architect may decline to certify payment and may withhold his Certificate in whole or in part, to the extent necessary reasonably to protect the Owner, if in his opinion he is unable to make representations to the Owner as provided in Subparagraph 9.4.2. If the Architect is unable to make representations to the Owner as provided in Subparagraph 9.4.2 and to certify payment in the amount of the Application, he will notify the Contractor as provided in Subparagraph 9.4.2. If the Contractor and the Architect cannot agree on a revised amount, the Architect will promptly issue a Certificate for Payment for the amount for which he is able to make such representations to the Owner. The Architect may also decline to certify payment or, because of subsequently discovered evidence or subsequent observations, he may nullify the whole or any part of any Certificate for Payment previously issued, to such extent as may be necessary in his opinion to protect the Owner from loss because of:

1. defective Work not remedied,

2. third party claims filed or reasonable evidence indicating probable filing of such claims,

3. failure of the Contractor to make payments properly to Subcontractors or for labor, materials or equipment,

4. reasonable evidence that the Work cannot be completed for the unpaid balance of the Contract Sum,

5. damage to the Owner or another contractor,

6. reasonable evidence that the Work will not be completed within the Contract Time, or

7. persistent failure to carry out the Work in accordance with the Contract Documents.

9.6.2   When the above grounds in Subparagraph 9.6.1 are removed, payment shall be made for amounts withheld because of them.

9.7   FAILURE OF PAYMENT

9.7.1   If the Architect does not issue a Certificate for Payment, through no fault of the Contractor, within seven days after receipt of the Contractor's Application for Payment, or if the Owner does not pay the Contractor within seven days after the date established in the Contract Documents any amount certified by the Architect or awarded by arbitration, then the Contractor may, upon seven additional days' written notice to the Owner and the Architect, stop the Work until payment of the amount owing has been received. The Contract Sum shall be increased by the amount of the Contractor's reasonable costs of shutdown, delay and start-up which shall be effected by appropriate Change Order in accordance with Paragraph 12.3.

9.8   SUBSTANTIAL COMPLETION

9.8.1   When the Contractor considers that the Work, or a designated portion thereof which is acceptable to the Owner, is substantially complete as defined in Subparagraph 8.1.3, the Contractor shall prepare for submission to the Architect a list of items to be completed or corrected. The failure to include any items on such list does not alter the responsibility of the contractor to complete all Work in accordance with the Contract Documents. When the Architect on the basis of an inspection determines that the Work or designated portion thereof is substantially complete, he will then prepare a Certificate of Substantial Completion which shall establish the Date of Substantial Completion, shall state the responsibilities of the Owner and the Contractor for security, maintenance, heat, utilities, damage to the Work, and insurance, and shall fix the time within which the Contractor shall complete the items listed therein. Warranties required by the Contract Documents shall commence on the Date of Substantial Completion of the Work or designated portion thereof unless otherwise provided in the Certificate of Substantial Completion. The Certificate of Substantial Completion shall be submitted to the Owner and the Contractor for their written acceptance of the responsibilities assigned to them in such Certificate.

9.8.2 Upon Substantial Completion of the Work or designated portion thereof and upon application by the Contractor and certification by the Architect, the Owner shall make payment, reflecting adjustment in retainage, if any, for such Work or portion thereof, as provided in the Contract Documents.

9.9 FINAL COMPLETION AND FINAL PAYMENT

9.9.1 Upon receipt of written notice that the Work is ready for final inspection and acceptance and upon receipt of a final Application for Payment, the Architect will promptly make such inspection and, when he finds the Work acceptable under the Contract Documents and the Contract fully performed, he will promptly issue a final Certificate for Payment stating that to the best of his knowledge, information and belief, and on the basis of his observations and inspections, the Work has been completed in accordance with the terms and conditions of the Contract Documents and that the entire balance found to be due the Contractor, and noted in said final Certificate, is due and payable. The Architect's final Certificate for Payment will constitute a further representation that the conditions precedent to the Contractor's being entitled to final payment as set forth in Subparagraph 9.9.2 have been fulfilled.

9.9.2 Neither the final payment nor the remaining retained percentage shall become due until the Contractor submits to the Architect (1) an affidavit that all payrolls bills for materials and equipment, and other indebtedness connected with the Work for which the Owner or his property might in any way be responsible, have been paid or otherwise satisfied, consent of surety, if any, to final payment and (3), if required by

the Owner, other data establishing payment or satisfaction of all such obligation s, such as receipts, releases and waivers of liens arising out of the Contract, to the extent and in such form as may be designated by the Owner. If any Subcontractor refuses to furnish a release or waiver required by the Owner, the Contractor may furnish a bond satisfactory to the Owner to indemnify him against any such lien. If any such lien remains unsatisfied after all payments are made, the Contractor shall refund to the Owner all moneys that the latter may be compelled to pay in discharging such lien, including all costs and reasonable attorneys' fees.

9.9.3 If, after Substantial Completion of the Work, final completion thereof is materially delayed through no fault of the Contractor or by the issuance of Change Orders affecting final completion, and the Architect so confirms, the Owner shall, upon application by the Contractor and certification by the Architect, and without terminating the Contract, make payment of the balance due for that portion of the Work fully completed and accepted. If the remaining balance for Work not fully completed or corrected is less than the retainage stipulated in the Contract Documents, and if bonds have been furnished as provided in Paragraph 7.5, the written consent of the surety to the payment of the balance due for that portion of the Work fully completed and accepted shall be submitted by the Contractor to the Architect prior to certification of such payment. Such payment shall be made under the terms and conditions governing final payment, except that it shall not constitute a waiver of claims.

9.9.4 The making of final payment shall constitute a waiver of all claims by the Owner except those arising from:

1. unsettled liens,

2. faulty of defective Work appearing after Substantial Completion,

3. failure of the Work to comply with the requirements of the Contract Documents, or

4. terms of any special warranties required by the Contract Documents

9.9.5 The acceptance of final payment shall constitute a waiver of all claims by the Contractor except those previously made in writing and identified by the Contractor as unsettled at the time of the final Application for Payment.

ARTICLE 10

PROTECTION OF PERSONS AND PROPERTY

10.1 SAFETY PRECAUTIONS AND PROGRAMS

10.1.1 The Contractor shall be responsible for initiating, maintaining and supervising all safety precautions and programs in connection with the Work.

10.1.2 SAFETY OF PERSONS AND PROPERTY

10.2.1 The Contractor shall take all reasonable precautions for the safety of, and shall provide all reasonable protection to prevent damage, injury or loss to:

1. all employees on the Work and all other persons who may be affected thereby;

2. all the Work and all materials and equipment to be incorporated therein, whether in storage on or off the site, under the care, custody or control of the Contractor or any of his Subcontractors or Sub-subcontractors: and

3. other property at the site or adjacent thereto, including trees, shrubs, lawns, walks, pavements, roadways, structures and utilities not designated for removal, relocation or replacement in the course of construction.

10.2.2 The Contractor shall give all notices and comply with all applicable laws, ordinances, rules, regulations and lawful orders of any public authority bearing on the safety of persons or property or their protection from damage, injury or loss.

10.2.3 The Contractor shall erect and maintain, as required by existing conditions and progress of the Work, all reasonable safeguards for safety and protection, including posting danger signs and other warnings against hazards, promulgating safety regulations and notifying owners and users of adjacent utilities.

10.2.4 When the use or storage of explosives or other hazardous materials or equipment is necessary for the execution of the Work, the Contractor shall exercise the utmost care and shall carry on such activities under the supervision of properly qualified personnel.

10.2.5 The Contractor shall promptly remedy all damage or loss (~~other than damage or less insured under Paragraph 11.3~~) to any property referred to in Clauses 10.2.1.2 and 10.2.1.3 caused in whole or in part by the Contractor, any Subcontractor, any Sub-subcontractor, or anyone directly or indirectly employed by any of them, or by anyone for whose acts any of them may be liable and for which the Contractor is responsible under Clauses 10.2.1.2 and 10.2.1.3, except damage or loss attributable to the acts or omissions of the Owner or Architect or anyone directly or indirectly employed by either of them, or by anyone for whose acts either of them may be liable, and not attributable to the fault or negligence of the Contractor. The foregoing obligations of the Contractor are in addition to his obligations under Paragraph 4.18.

10.2.6 The Contractor shall designate a responsible member of his organization at the site whose duty shall be the prevention of accidents. This person shall be the Contractor's superintendent unless otherwise designated by the Contractor in writing to the Owner and the Architect.

10.2.7 The Contractor shall not load or permit any part of the Work to be loaded so as to endanger its safety.

10.3 EMERGENCIES

10.3.1 In any emergency affecting the safety of persons or property, the Contractor shall act, at his discretion, to prevent threatened damage, injury or loss. Any additional compensation or extension of time claimed by the Contractor on account of emergency work shall be determined as provided in Article 12 for Changes in the Work.

ARTICLE 11

INSURANCE

11.1   CONTRACTOR'S LIABILITY INSURANCE

11.1   The Contractor shall purchase and maintain such insurance as will protect him from claims set forth below which may arise out of or result from the Contractor's operations under the Contract, whether such operations be by himself or by any Subcontractor or by anyone directly or indirectly employed by any of them, or by anyone for whose acts any of them may be liable:

1.   claims under workers' or workmen's compensation, disability benefit and other similar employee benefit acts;

2.   claims for damages because of bodily injury, occupational sickness or disease, or death of his employees;

3.   claims for damages because of bodily injury, sickness or disease, or death of any person other than his employees;

4.   claims for damages insured by usual personal injury liability coverage which are sustained (1) by any person as a result of an offense directly or indirectly related to the employment of such person by the Contractor, or (2) by any other person;

5.   claims for damages, other than to the Work itself, because of injury to or destruction of tangible property, including loss of use resulting therefrom; and

6.   claims for damages because of bodily injury or death of any person or property damage arising out of the ownership, maintenance or use of any motor vehicle.

11.1.2 The insurance required by Subparagraph 11.1.1 shall be written for not less than any limits of liability specified in the Contract Documents, or required by law, whichever is greater. Liability insurance shall be in amount of not less than $1,000,000 per occurrence.

11.1.3 The insurance required by Subparagraph 11.1.1 shall include contractual liability insurance applicable to the Contractor's obligations under Paragraph 4.18. The insurance shall include the Owner as an additional insured.

11.1.4 Certificates of Insurance acceptable to the Owner shall be filed with the Owner prior to commencement of the Work. These Certificates shall contain a provision that coverages afforded under the policies will not be cancelled until at least thirty days' prior written notice has been given to the Owner.

11.2   OWNER'S LIABILITY INSURANCE

11.2.1 ~~The Owner shall be responsible for purchasing and maintaining his own liability insurance and, at his option, may purchase and maintain such insurance as will protect him against claims which may arise from operations under the Contract.~~

11.3   PROPERTY INSURANCE

11.3.1 Unless otherwise provided, the Owner shall purchase and maintain property insurance upon the entire Work at the site to the full insurable value thereof. This insurance shall include the interests of the Owner, the Contractor, Subcontractors and Sub-subcontractors in the Work and shall insure against the perils of fire and extended coverage and shall include "all risk" insurance for physical loss or damage including, without duplication of coverage, theft, vandalism and malicious mischief. If the Owner does not intend to purchase such insurance for the full insurable value of the entire Work, he shall inform the Contractor in writing prior to commencement of the Work. The Contractor may then effect insurance which will protect the interests of himself, his Subcontractors and the Sub-subcontractors in the Work, and by appropriate Change Order the cost thereof shall be charged to the Owner. If the Contractor is damaged by failure of the Owner to purchase or maintain such insurance and to so notify the

Contractor, then the Owner shall bear all reasonable costs properly attributable thereto. If not covered under the all risk insurance or otherwise provided in the Contract Documents, the Contractor shall effect and maintain similar property insurance on portions of the Work stored off the site or in transit when such portions of the Work are to be included in an Application for Payment under Subparagraph 9.3.2.

11.3.2 The Owner shall purchase and maintain such boiler and machinery insurance as may be required by the Contract Documents or by law. This insurance shall include the interests of the Owner, the Contractor, Subcontractors and Sub-subcontractors in the Work.

11.3.3 Any loss insured under Subparagraph 11.3.1 is to be adjusted with the Owner and made payable to the Owner as trustee for the insureds, as their interests may appear, subject to the requirements of any applicable mortgagee clause and of Subparagraph 11.3.8. The Contractor shall pay each Subcontractor a just share of any insurance moneys received by the Contractor, and by appropriate agreement, written where legally required for validity, shall require each Subcontractor to make payments to his Sub-subcontractors in similar manner.

11.3.4 The Owner shall file a copy of all policies with the Contractor before an exposure to loss may occur.

11.3.5 If the Contractor requests in writing that insurance for risks other than those described in Subparagraphs 11.3.1 and 11.3.2 or other special hazards be included in the property insurance policy, the Owner shall, if possible, include such insurance, and the cost thereof shall be charged to the Contractor by appropriate Change Order.

11.3.6 ~~The Owner and Contractor waive all rights against (1) each other and the Subcontractors, Sub-subcontractors, agents and employees each of the other, and (2) the Architect and separate contractors, if any, and their subcontractors, sub-subcontractors, agents and employees, for damages caused by fire or other perils to the extent covered by insurance~~

~~obtained pursuant to this Paragraph 11.2 or any other property insurance applicable to the Work, except such rights as they may have to the proceeds of such insurance held by the Owner as trustee. The foregoing waiver afforded the Architect, his agents and employees shall not extend to the liability imposed by Subparagraph 4.18.2. The Owner or the Contractor, as appropriate, shall require of the Architect, separate contractors, Subcontractors and Sub-subcontractors by appropriate agreements, written where legally required for validity, similar waivers each in favor of all other parties enumerated in this Subparagraph 11.2.6.~~

11.3.7 If required in writing by any party in interest, the Owner as trustee shall, upon the occurrence of an insured loss, give bond for the proper performance of his duties. He shall deposit in a separate account any money so received, and he shall distribute it in accordance with such agreement as the parties in interest may reach, or in accordance with such agreement as the parties in interest may reach, or in accordance with an award by arbitration in which case the procedure shall be as provided in Paragraph 7.9. If after such loss no other special agreement is made, replacement of damaged work shall be covered by an appropriate Change Order.

11.3.8 The Owner as trustee shall have power to adjust and settle any loss with the insurers unless one of the parties in interest shall object in writing within five days after the occurrence of loss to the Owner's exercise of this power, and if such objection be made, arbitrators shall be chosen as provided in Paragraph 7.9. The Owner as trustee shall, in that case, make settlement with the insurers in accordance with the directions of such arbitrators. If distribution of the insurance proceeds by arbitration is required, the arbitrators will direct such distribution.

11.3.9 If the Owner finds it necessary to occupy or use a portion or portions of the Work prior to Substantial Completion thereof, such occupancy or use shall not commence prior to a time mutually agreed to by the Owner and Contractor and to which the insurance company or companies providing the property insurance have consented by endorsement to the policy or policies. This insurance shall not be cancelled or lapsed on account of such partial occupancy or use. Consent of the Contractor and of the insurance company or companies to such occupancy or use shall not be unreasonably withheld.

11.4   LOSS OF USE INSURANCE

11.4.1 The Owner, at his option, may purchase and maintain such insurance as will insure him against loss of use of his property due to fire or other hazards, however caused. ~~The Owner waives all rights of action against the Contractor for loss of use of his property, including consequential losses due to fire or other hazards however caused, to the extent covered by insurance under this Paragraph 11.4.~~

ARTICLE 12
CHANGES IN THE WORK

12.1   CHANGE ORDERS

12.1.1 A Change Order is a written order to the Contractor signed by the Owner and the Architect, issued after execution of the Contract, authorizing a change in the Work or an adjustment in the Contract Sum or the Contract Time. The Contract Sum and the Contract Time may be changed only by Change Order. A Change Order signed by the Contractor indicates his agreement therewith, including the adjustment in the Contract Sum or the Contract Time.

12.1.2 The Owner, without invalidating the Contract, may order changes in the Work within the general scope of the Contract consisting of additions, deletions or other revisions, the Contract Sum and the Contract Time being adjusted accordingly. All such changes in the Work shall be authorized by Change Order, and shall be performed under the applicable conditions of the Contract Documents.

12.1.3 The cost or credit to the Owner resulting from a change in the Work shall be determined in one or more of the following ways:

1. by mutual acceptance of a lump sum properly itemized and supported by sufficient substantiating data to permit evaluation;

2. by unit prices stated in the Contract Documents or subsequently agreed upon;

3. by cost to be determined in a manner agreed upon by the parties and a mutually acceptable fixed or percentage fee; or

4. by the method provided in Subparagraph 12.1.4.

12.1.4 If none of the methods set forth in Clauses 12.1.3.1, 12.1.3.2 or 12.1.3.3 is agreed upon, the Contractor, provided he receives a written order signed by the Owner, shall promptly proceed with the Work involved. The cost of such Work shall then be determined by the Architect on the basis of the reasonable expenditures and savings of those performing the Work attributable to the change, including, in the case of an increase in the Contract Sum, a reasonable allowance for overhead and profit. In such case, and also under Clauses 12.1.3.3 and 12.1.3.4 above, the Contractor shall keep and present, in such form as the Architect may prescribe, an itemized accounting together with appropriate supporting data for inclusion in a Change Order. Unless otherwise provided in the Contract Documents, cost shall be limited to the following: cost of materials, including social security, old age and unemployment insurance, and fringe benefits required by agreement or custom; workers' or workmen's compensation insurance; bond premiums; rental value of equipment and machinery; and the additional costs of supervision and field office personnel directly attributable to the change. Pending final determination of cost to the Owner, payments on account shall be made on the Architect's Certificate for Payment. The amount of credit to be allowed by the Contractor to the Owner for any deletion or change which results in a net decrease in the Contract Sum will be the amount of the actual net cost as confirmed by the Architect. When both additions and credits covering related Work or substitutions are involved in any one change, the allowance for overhead and profit shall be figured on the basis of the net increase, if any, with respect to that change.

12.1.5 If unit prices are stated in the Contract Documents or subsequently agreed upon, and if the quantities originally contemplated are so changed in a proposed Change Order that application of the Agreed unit prices to the quantities of Work proposed will cause substantial inequity to the Owner or the Contractor, the applicable unit prices shall be equitably adjusted.

12.2 CONCEALED CONDITIONS

12.2.1 Should concealed conditions encountered in the performance of the Work below the surface of the ground or should concealed or unknown conditions in an existing structure be at variance with the conditions indicated by the Contract Documents, or should unknown physical conditions below the surface of the ground or should concealed or unknown conditions in an existing structure of an unusual nature, differing materially from those ordinarily encountered, the Contract Sum shall be equitably adjusted by Change Order upon claim by either party made within twenty days after the first observance of the conditions.

12.3 CLAIMS FOR ADDITIONAL COST

12.3.1 If the Contractor wishes to make a claim for an increase in the Contract Sum, he shall give the Architect written notice thereof within twenty days after the occurrence of the event giving rise to such claim. This notice shall be given by the Contractor before proceeding to execute the Work, except in an emergency endangering life or property in which case the Contractor shall proceed in accordance with Paragraph 10.3. No such claim shall be valid unless so made. If the Owner and the Contractor cannot agree on the amount of the adjustment in the Contract Sum, it shall be determined by the Architect. Any change in the Contract Sum resulting from such claim shall be authorized by Change Order.

12.3.2 If the Contractor claims that additional cost is involved because of, but not limited to, (1) any written interpretation pursuant to Subparagraph 2.2.8, (2) any order by the Owner

to stop the Work pursuant to Paragraph 3.3 where the Contractor was not at fault, (3) any written order for a minor change in the Work issued pursuant to Paragraph 12.4, or (4) failure of payment by the Owner pursuant to Paragraph 9.7, the Contractor shall make such claim as provided in Subparagraph 12.3.1.

12.4 MINOR CHANGES IN THE WORK

12.4.1 The Architect will have authority to order minor changes in the Work not involving an adjustment in the Contract Sum or an extension of the Contract Time and not inconsistent with the intent of the Contract Documents. Such changes shall be effected by written order, and shall be binding on the Owner and the Contractor. The Contractor shall carry out such written orders promptly.

ARTICLE 13

UNCOVERING AND CORRECTION OF WORK

13.1 UNCOVERING OF WORK

13.1.1 If any portion of the Work should be covered contrary to the request of the Architect or to requirements specifically expressed in the Contract Documents, it must, if required in writing by the Architect, be uncovered for his observation and shall be replaced at the Contractor's expense.

13.1.2 If any other portion of the Work has been covered which the Architect has not specifically requested to observe prior to being covered, the Architect may request to see such Work and it shall be uncovered by the Contractor. If such Work be found in accordance with the Contract Documents, the cost of uncovering and replacement shall, by appropriate Change Order, be charged to the Owner. If such Work be found not in accordance with the Contract Documents, the cost of uncovering and replacement shall, by appropriate Change Order, be charged to the Owner. If such Work be found not in accordance with the Contract Documents, the Contractor shall pay such costs unless it be found that this condition was caused by the Owner or a separate contractor as provided in Article 6, in which event the Owner shall be responsible for the payment of such costs.

13.2 CORRECTION OF WORK

13.2.1 The Contractor shall promptly correct all Work rejected by the Architect as defective or as failing to conform to the Contract Documents whether observed before or after Substantial Completion and whether or not fabricated, installed or completed. The Contractor shall bear all costs of correcting such rejected Work, including compensation for the Architect's additional services made necessary thereby.

13.2.2 If, within one year after the Date of Substantial Completion of the Work or designated portion thereof or within one year after acceptance by the Owner of designated equipment or within such longer period of time as may be permitted by law or by the terms of any applicable special warranty required by the Contract Documents, any of the Work is found to be defective or not in accordance with the Contract Documents, the Contractor shall correct it promptly after receipt of a written notice from the Owner to do so unless the Owner has previously given the Contractor a written acceptance of such condition. This obligation shall survive termination of the Contract. The Owner shall give such notice promptly after discovery of the condition.

13.2.3 The Contractor shall remove from the site all portions of the Work which are defective or nonconforming and which have not been corrected under Subparagraphs 4.5.1, 13.2.1 and 13.2.2, unless removal is waived by the Owner.

13.2.4 If the Contractor fails to correct defective or non-conforming Work as provided in Subparagraphs 4.5.1, 13.2.1 and 13.2.2, the Owner may correct it in accordance with Paragraph 3.4.

13.2.5 If the Contractor does not proceed with the correction of such defective or non-conforming Work within a reasonable time fixed by written notice from the Architect, the Owner may remove it and may store the materials or equipment at the expense of the Contractor. If

the Contractor does not pay the cost of such removal and storage within ten days thereafter, the Owner may upon ten additional days' written notice sell such Work at auction or at private sale and shall account for the net proceeds thereof, after deducting all the costs that should have been borne by the Contractor, including compensation for the Architect's additional services made necessary thereby. If such proceeds of sale do not cover all costs which the Contractor should have borne, the difference shall be charged to the Contractor and an appropriate Change Order shall be issued. If the payments then or thereafter due the Contractor are not sufficient to cover such amount, the Contractor shall pay the difference to the Owner.

13.2.6 The Contractor shall bear the cost of making good all work of the Owner or separate contractors destroyed or damaged by such correction or removal.

13.2.7 Nothing contained in this Paragraph 3.2 shall be construed to establish a period of limitation with respect to any other obligation which the Contractor might have under the Contract Documents, including Paragraph 4.5 hereof. The establishment of the time period of one year after the Date of Substantial Completion or such longer period of time as may be permitted by law or by the terms of any warranty required by the Contract Documents relates only to the specific obligation of the Contractor to correct the Work, and has no relationship to the time within which his obligation to comply with the Contract Documents may be sought to be enforced, nor to the time within which proceedings may be commenced to establish the Contractor's liability with respect to his obligations other than specifically to correct the Work.

13.3 ACCEPTANCE OF DEFECTIVE OR NON- CONFORMING WORK

13.3.1 If the Owner prefers to accept defective or non-conforming Work, he may do so instead of requiring its removal and correction, in which case a Change Order will be issued to reflect a reduction in the Contract Sum where appropriate and equitable. Such adjustment shall be effected whether or not final payment has been made.

ARTICLE 14

TERMINATION OF THE CONTRACT

14.1 TERMINATION BY THE CONTRACTOR

14.1.1 If the Work is stopped for a period of thirty days under an order of any court or other public authority having jurisdiction, or as a result of an act of government, such as a declaration of a national emergency making materials unavailable, through no act or fault of the Contractor or a Subcontractor or their agents or employees or any other persons performing any of the Work under a contract with the Contractor, or if the Work should be stopped for a period of thirty days by the Contractor because the Architect has not issued a Certificate for Payment as provided in Paragraph 9.7 or because the Owner has not made payment thereon as provided in Paragraph 9.7, then the Contractor may, upon seven additional days' written notice to the Owner and the Architect, terminate the Contract and recover from the Owner payment for all Work.

14.2 TERMINATION BY THE OWNER

14.2.1 If the Contractor is adjudged a bankrupt, or if he makes a general assignment for the benefit of his creditors, or if a receiver is appointed on account of his insolvency, or if he persistently or repeatedly refuses or fails, except in cases for which extension of time is provided to supply enough properly skilled workmen or proper materials, or if he fails to make prompt payment to Subcontractors or for materials or labor, or persistently disregards laws, ordinances, rules, regulations or orders of any public authority having jurisdiction, or otherwise is guilty of a substantial violation of a provision of the Contract Documents, or fails to achieve Substantial Completion of the Work by the date required under Article 3 of the Standard Form of Agreement Between Owner and Contractor entered into by the parties of which this is a part, then the Owner, upon certification by the Architect that sufficient cause exists to justify such action, may, without prejudice to any right or remedy and after giving the Contractor and his surety, if any, seven days' written notice, terminate the employment of the Contractor and take possession of the site and of all materials, equipment, tools, construction equipment and machinery thereon owned by the Contractor and may finish the Work by whatever method he may deem expedient. In such case the Contractor shall not be entitled to receive any further payment until the Work is finished.

14.2.2 If the unpaid balance of the Contract Sum exceeds the costs of finishing the Work, including compensation for the Architect's additional services made necessary thereby, such excess shall be paid to the Contractor. If such costs exceed the unpaid balance, the Contractor shall pay the difference to the Owner. The amount to be paid to the Contractor or to the Owner, as the case may be, shall be certified by the Architect, upon application, in the manner provided in Paragraph 9.4, and this obligation for payment shall survive the termination of the Contract.

INSTRUCTION SHEET   AIA DOCUMENT   A111a

FOR AIA DOCUMENT A111, STANDARD FORM OF AGREEMENT BETWEEN OWNER AND CONTRACTOR where the basis of payment is the COST OF THE WORK PLUS A FEE—1978 EDITION

A. GENERAL INFORMATION:

AIA Document A111, Standard Form or Agreement Between Owner and Contractor, is for use where the basis of payment to the Contractor is the cost of the Work plus a fixed or percentage fee. The 1978 Edition has been prepared for use in conjunction with the 1976 Edition of AIA Document A201, General Conditions of the Contract for Construction and contains provisions for stipulating a Guaranteed Maximum Cost. Although the Cost Plus Fee Arrangement lacks the financial certainty of a lump sum agreement, it may be desirable when fixed prices on portions of the Work cannot be obtained, or when construction must be started before Drawings and Specifications are completed, as well as under other circumstances.

B. CHANGES FROM THE PREVIOUS EDITION:

Provisions which have been revised in or added to the 1978 Edition of the Cost Plus Fee Owner-Contractor Agreement are listed below:

1. ARTICLE 4—TIME OF COMMENCEMENT AND SUBSTANTIAL COMPLETION:

The word "SUBSTANTIAL" has been added to the article name. The General Conditions, AIA Document A201, 1976 Edition, make it clear that the Contract Time runs until the Date of Substantial Completion; the Owner should be aware that an additional period of time will be required to reach final completion.

Paragraph 4.1: Revised to clarify that the Contract Time is subject to Owner-authorized adjustments by Change Order.

2. ARTICLE 7—CHANGES IN THE WORK:

Paragraph 7.1: Revised to reference the Contract Documents rather than just the General Conditions, in determining the procedure for and the amount of Change Orders.

3. ARTICLE 8—COSTS TO BE REIMBURSED:

Subparagraph 8.1.16: A parenthetical statement has been added calling attention to the space for desired modifications.

4. ARTICLE 9—COSTS NOT TO BE REIMBURSED:

Subparagraph 9.1.4: New subparagraph. Rental costs not specifically provided for in Subparagraph 8.1.8 or in modifications thereto are not to be reimbursed.

5. ARTICLE 11—SUBCONTRACTS AND OTHER AGREEMENTS:

Article modified to clarify that agreements other than subcontracts are also subject to Article 11.

6. ARTICLE 13—APPLICATIONS FOR PAYMENT:

Paragraph 13.1 Revised to clarify that the Owner and Architect may require such supporting data as necessary to certify the Contractor's right to payment.

7. ARTICLE 14—PAYMENTS TO THE CONTRACTOR:

Paragraph 4.1: Revised pursuant to the 1976 Edition of A201 to clarify that the Architect will take appropriate action in response to the Contractor's Application for Payment. The Owner and Contractor should be aware that the Architect will recommend payment only after the Contractor's right to payments has been substantiated.

Subparagraph 14.1.1: A new provision added to clarify that the Architect must and does rely on the information provided by the Contractor in recommending payment. The Architect is not expected to confirm that the Contractor has actually paid all expenses incurred.

Paragraph 14.3: A new provision, conforming with the 1976 Edition of A201, to allow prior agreement on a rate of interest for overdue payments. A parenthetical statement, calling attention to Federal and state laws applicable to interest provisions, has also been added.

8. ARTICLE 16—MISCELLANEOUS PROVISIONS:

Paragraph 16.1: Revised to reference the Contract Documents rather than just the General Conditions.

C. COMPLETING THE FORM:

(NOTE: Prospective bidders should be made aware of any additional provisions which may be included in A111, such as liquidated damages, retainage, or payment for stored materials, by an appropriate notice in the Bidding Documents.)

1. Cover Page

The names of the Owner and the Architect should be shown in the same form as in the other Contract Documents include the full legal or corporate names under which the Owner and Contractor are entering the Agreement.

2. ARTICLE 2—THE WORK:

3. ARTICLE 4—TIME OF COMMENCEMENT AND SUBSTANTIAL COMPLETION:

The following items should be included as appropriate:

a. Date of commencement of the Work: This should not be earlier than the date of execution of the Contract. When time of performance is to be strictly enforced, the statement of starting time should be carefully considered. At the end of the first line, enter either the specific date of commencement of the Work, or if a notice to proceed is to be used, enter the words, "on the date stipulated in the notice to proceed."

b. Substantial Completion of the Work: Substantial Completion of the Work may be expressed as a number of days (preferably calendar days) or as a specified date.

c. Provision for liquidated damages: If liquidated damages are to be assessed because delayed construction will result in the Owner actually suffering loss, the entire provision for liquidated damages should be entered in the instructions to bidders as well as the Agreement. This provision should be drafted by the Owner's attorney. Liquidated damages are not a penalty to be inflicted on the Contractor, but must bear an actual and reasonably estimated relationship to the loss of the Owner if the building is not completed on time: for example, the cost per day of renting space to house students if a dormitory cannot be occupied when needed, additional financing costs, loss of profits, etc.

4. **ARTICLE 5—COST OF THE WORK AND GUARANTEED MAXIMUM COST:**

Any incentive provisions for distribution of savings under a Guaranteed Maximum Cost should be included in Article 5. Delete Paragraph 5.2 if no maximum cost is established.

5. **ARTICLE 6—CONTRACTOR'S FEE:**

The Contractor's fee may be stated as a stipulated sum or as a percentage of Cost of the Work. Fee adjustments adding to and subtracting from the Contractor's fee may be related to the cost of the Change or some other means.

6. **ARTICLE 8—COSTS TO BE REIMBURSED and ARTICLE 9—COSTS NOT TO BE REIMBURSED:**

All costs which are established as reimbursed or expressly not reimbursable should be stated in Articles 8 and 9.

An appropriate provision should be included in Article 8 if the Contractor's overhead costs associated with corrective work are to be reimbursed, when such overhead costs are incurred after final payment.

7. **ARTICLE 14—PAYMENTS TO THE CONTRACTOR:**

Due dates for payments should be established in consideration of the time required for the Contractor to prepare an Application for Payment, for the Architect to take appropriate action, and for the Owner to make payment, within the time limits set in Article 9 of A201 and in this Article of A111. Note that the Architect does not "certify" payment under this contract form, and if the Architect uses AIA Document G702. Application and Certificate for Payment, the certification provisions should be deleted, not only from G702. Application and Certificate for Payment, the certification provisions should be deleted, not only from G702, but also from the Owner-Architect Agreement.

8. **ARTICLE 16—MISCELLANEOUS PROVISIONS:**

An accurate, detailed enumeration of all Contract Documents must be made in this Article.

9. **Signatures:**

Subparagraph 1.2.1 of AIA Document A201 states that the Contract Documents shall be executed in not less than triplicate by the Owner and the Contractor. The Agreement should be executed by the parties in their capacities as individuals, partners, officers, etc., as appropriate.

D. REPRODUCTION:

AIA Document A111 is a copyrighted document, and may not be reproduced or excerpted from in substantial part without the express written permission of AIA. Purchasers of A111 are hereby entitled to reproduce a maximum of ten copies of the completed or executed document for use only in connection with the particular Project. AIA will not permit the reproduction of this document in blank, or the use of substantial portions of, or language from, this Document, except upon written request and after receipt of written permission from AIA.

THE AMERICAN INSTITUTE OF ARCHITECTS

AIA Document A111

Standard Form of Agreement Between Owner and Contractor

where the basis of payment is the

COST OF THE WORK PLUS A FEE

20__ EDITION

THIS DOCUMENT HAS IMPORTANT LEGAL CONSEQUENCES; CONSULTATION WITH AN ATTORNEY IS ENCOURAGED WITH RESPECT TO ITS COMPLETION OR MODIFICATION

Use only with the 20__ Edition of AIA Document A201, General Conditions of the Contract for Construction.

This document has been approved and endorsed by The Associated General Contractors of America

AGREEMENT

made as of the tenth (10th) day of August in the year of Two Thousand and _____.

BETWEEN the Owner: Ms. Michelle Greenwood, President, for Area Development corporation and the Contractor: John Ross, President, for Ross Construction Company

The project: Conversion of the Little Sisters of the Poor Convent owned by Area

Development Corporation into forty (40) luxury condominiums

the Architect: Bob Johnson

The Owner and the Contractor agree as set forth below.

ARTICLE 1

THE CONTRACT DOCUMENTS

1.1 The Contract Documents consist of this Agreement the Conditions of the Contract; General Supplementary and other Conditions, the Drawings, the Specifications, all Addenda issued prior to and all Modifications issued after execution of this Agreement. These form the Contract, and all are as fully a part of the Contract as if attached to this Agreement or repeated herein. An enumeration of the Contract Documents appears in Article 16. If anything in the Contract Documents is inconsistent with this Agreement, the Agreement shall govern.

ARTICLE 2

THE WORK

2.1 The Contractor shall perform all the Work required by the Contract Documents for alterations and additions to the owners' property bounded by North Plum, North Harvie, West Main Streets, and Floyd Avenue, Nita City, Nita, otherwise known as the Little Sisters of the Poor Convent. Any discrepancy or ambiguity in the Contract Documents shall be subject to interpretation by the Architect as provided herein.

ARTICLE 3

THE CONTRACTOR'S DUTIES AND STATUS

3.1 The Contractor accepts the relationship of trust and confidence established between him and the Owner by this Agreement. He covenants with the Owner to furnish his best skill and judgment and to cooperate with the Architect in furthering the interests of the Owner. He agrees to furnish efficient business administration and superintendence and to use his best efforts to furnish at all times an adequate supply of workmen and materials, and to perform the Work in the best way and in the most expeditious and economical manner consistent with the interests of the Owner.

ARTICLE 4

TIME OF COMMENCEMENT AND SUBSTANTIAL COMPLETION

4.1 The work to be performed under this Contract shall be commenced forthwith and, subject to authorized adjustments, Substantial Completion shall be achieved not later than six (6) months after the (Here insert any special provisions for liquidated damages relating to failure to complete on time.) contractor has been notified as to the final design of a unit.

ARTICLE 5

COST OF THE WORK AND GUARANTEED MAXIMUM COST

5.1 The Owner agrees to reimburse the Contractor for the Cost of the Work as defined in Article 8. Such reimbursement shall be in addition to the Contractor's Fee stipulated in Article 6.

5.2 The maximum cost to the Owner, including the Cost of the Work and Contractor's Fee, is guaranteed not to exceed the sum of N/A dollars, $. Such Guaranteed Maximum Cost shall be increased or decreased for Changes in the Work as provided in Article 7.

Here insert any provision for distribution of any savings. Delete Paragraph 5.2 if there is no Guaranteed Maximum Costs.

ARTICLE 6

CONTRACTOR'S FEE

6.1 In consideration of the performance of the Contract, the Owner agrees to pay the Contractor in current funds as compensation for his services a Contractor's Fee as follows:

10% of the cost of work as defined in Article 8 of each condominium unit. In addition, the owner agrees to pay the contractor 10% of the cost of work as defined in Article 8 for work done on the common areas.

6.2 For Changes in the Work, the Contractor's Fee shall be adjusted as follows:

The Contractor shall be paid 10% of the cost of work as to changes authorized by the owner. (See General Conditions Section of 1976 Edition AIA Document A 201).

6.3 The Contractor shall be paid Eighty percent (80%) of the proportional amount of his Fee with each completion of a unit and the balance of his Fee shall be paid at the time of final payment.

ARTICLE 7

CHANGES IN THE WORK

7.1 The Owner may make Changes in the Work as provided in the Contract Documents. The Contractor shall be reimbursed for Changes in the Work on the basis of Cost of the Work as defined in Article 8.

7.2 The Contractor's Fee for Changes in the Work shall be as set forth in Paragraph 6.2, or in the absence of specific provisions therein, shall be adjusted by negotiation on the basis or the Fee established for the original Work.

ARTICLE 8

COSTS TO BE REIMBURSED

8.1 The term Cost of the Work shall mean costs necessarily incurred in the proper performance of the Work and paid by the Contractor. Such costs shall be at rates not higher than the standard paid in the locality of the Work except with prior consent of the Owner, and shall include the items set forth below in this Article 8.

8.1.1 Wages paid for labor in the direct employ of the contractor in the performance of the Work under applicable collective bargaining agreements, or under a salary or wage schedule agreed upon by the Owner and Contractor, and including such welfare or other benefits, if any, as may be payable with respect thereto.

8.1.2 Salaries of Contractor's personnel when stationed at the field office, in whatever capacity employed. Personnel engaged at shops or on the road, in expediting the production or transportation of materials or equipment, shall be considered as stationed at the field office and their salaries paid for that portion of their time spent on this Work.

8.1.3 Cost of contributions, assessments or taxes incurred during the performance of the Work for such items as unemployment compensation and social security, insofar as such cost is based on wages, salaries, or other remuneration paid to employees of the Contractor and included in the Cost of the Work under Subparagraphs 8.1.1 and 8.1.2.

8.1.4 The portion of reasonable travel and subsistence expenses of the Contractor or of his officers or employees incurred while traveling in discharge of duties connected with the Work.

8.1.5 Cost of all materials, supplies and equipment incorporated in the Work, including costs of transportation thereof.

8.1.6 Payments made by the Contractor to Subcontractors for Work performed pursuant to Subcontracts under this Agreement.

8.1.7 Cost including transportation and maintenance of all materials, supplies, equipment, temporary facilities and hand tools not owned by the workers, which are consumed in the performance of the Work, and cost less salvage value on such items used but not consumed which remain the property of the Contractor.

8.1.8 Rental charges of all necessary machinery and equipment, exclusive of hand tools, used at the site of the Work, whether rented from the Contractor or others, including installation, minor repairs and replacements, dismantling, removal, transportation and delivery costs thereof, at rental charges consistent with those prevailing in the area.

8.1.9 Cost of premiums for all bonds and insurance which the Contractor is required by the Contract Documents to purchase and maintain.

8.1.10 Sales, use or similar taxes related to the Work and for which the Contractor is required by the Contract Documents to purchase and maintain.

8.1.11 Permit fees, royalties, damages for infringement of patents and costs of defending suits therefor, and deposits lost for causes other than the Contractor's negligence.

8.1.12 Losses and expenses, not compensated by insurance or otherwise, sustained by the Contractor in connection with the Work, provided they have resulted from causes other than the fault or neglect of the Contractor. Such losses shall include settlements made with the written consent and approval of the Owner. No such losses and expenses shall be included in the Cost of the Work for the purpose of determining the Contractor's Fee. If, however, such loss requires reconstruction and the Contractor is placed in charge thereof, he shall be paid for his services a Fee proportionate to that stated in Paragraph 6.1.

8.1.13 Minor expenses such as telegrams, long distance telephone calls, telephone service at the site, expressage, and similar petty cash items in connection with the Work.

8.1.14 Cost of removal of all debris.

8.1.15 Cost incurred due to an emergency affecting the safety of persons and property.

8.1.16 Other costs incurred in the performance of the Work if and to the extent approved in advance in writing by the Owner.

ARTICLE 9

COSTS NOT TO BE REIMBURSED

9.1 The term Cost of the Work shall not include any of the items set forth below in this Article 9.

9.1.1 Salaries or other compensation of the Contractor's personnel at the Contractor's principal office and branch offices.

9.1.2 Expenses of the Contractor's principal and branch offices other than the field office.

9.1.3   Any part of the Contractor's capital expenses, including interest on the Contractor's capital employed for the Work.

9.1.4   Except as specifically provided for in Subparagraph 8.1.8 or in modifications thereto, rental costs of machinery and equipment.

9.1.5   Overhead or general expenses of any kind, except as may be expressly included in Article 8.

9.1.6   Costs due to the negligence of the Contractor, any Subcontractor, anyone directly or indirectly employed by any of them, or for whose acts any of them may be liable, including but not limited to the correction of defective or nonconforming Work, disposal of materials and equipment wrongly supplied, or making good any damage to property.

9.1.7   The cost of any item not specifically and expressly included in the items described in Article 8.

9.1.8   Costs in excess of the Guaranteed Maximum Cost, if any, as set forth in Article 5 and adjusted pursuant to Article 7.

ARTICLE 10

DISCOUNTS, REBATES AND REFUNDS

10.1   All cash discounts shall accrue to the Contractor unless the Owner deposits funds with the Contractor with which to make payments in which case the cash discounts shall accrue to the Owner. All trade discounts, rebates and refunds, and all returns from sale of surplus materials and equipment shall accrue to the Owner, and the Contractor shall make provisions so that they can be secured.

ARTICLE 11

SUBCONTRACTS AND OTHER AGREEMENTS

11.1   All portions of the Work that the Contractor's organization does not perform shall be performed under Subcontracts or by other appropriate agreement with the Contractor. The Contractor shall request bids from Subcontractors and shall deliver such bids to the Architect. The Owner will then determine, with the advice of the Contractor and subject to the reasonable objection of the Architect, which bids will be accepted.

11.2   All Subcontracts shall conform to the requirements of the Contract Documents. Subcontracts awarded on the basis of the cost of such work plus a fee shall also be subject to the provisions of this Agreement insofar as applicable.

ARTICLE 12

ACCOUNTING RECORDS

12.1   The Contractor shall check all materials, equipment and labor entering into the Work and shall keep such full and detailed accounts as may be necessary for proper financial management under this Agreement, and the system shall be satisfactory to the Owner. The Owner shall be afforded access to all the Contractor's records, books correspondence, instructions, drawings, receipts, vouchers, memoranda and similar data relating to this Contract, and the Contractor shall preserve all such records for a period of three years, or for such longer period as may be required by law, after the final payment.

ARTICLE 13

APPLICATIONS FOR PAYMENT

13.1 The Contractor shall, at least ten days before each payment falls due, deliver to the Architect an itemized statement, notarized if required, showing in complete detail all moneys paid out or costs incurred by him on account of the Cost of the Work during the previous month for which he is to be reimbursed under Article 5 and the amount of the Contractor's Fee due as provided in Article 6, together with payrolls for all labor and such other data supporting the Contractor's right to payment for Subcontracts or materials as the Owner or the Architect may require.

ARTICLE 14

PAYMENTS TO THE CONTRACTOR

14.1 The Architect will review the Contractor's Applications for Payment and will promptly take appropriate action thereon as provided in the Contract Documents. Such amount as he may recommend for payment shall be payable by the Owner not later than the 15th day of the month.

14.1.1 In taking action on the Contractor's Applications for Payment, the Architect shall be entitled to rely on the accuracy and completeness of the information furnished by the Contractor and shall not be deemed to represent that he has made audits of the supporting data, exhaustive or continuous on-site inspections or that he has made any examination to ascertain how or for what purposes the Contractor has used the moneys previously paid on account of the Contract.

14.2 Final payment, constituting the entire unpaid balance of the Cost of the Work and of the Contractor's Fee, shall be paid by the Owner to the Contractor days after Substantial Completion of the Work unless otherwise stipulated in the Certificate of Substantial Completion, provided the Work has been completed, the Contract fully performed, and final payment has been recommended by the Architect.

14.3 Payments due and unpaid under the Contract Documents shall bear interest from the date payment is due at the rate entered below, or in the absence thereof, at the legal rate prevailing at the place of the Project.

Here insert any rate of interest agreed upon.

ARTICLE 15

TERMINATION OF CONTRACT

15.1 The Contract may be terminated by the Contractor as provided in the Contract Documents.

15.2 If the Owner terminates the Contract as provided in the Contract Documents, he shall reimburse the Contractor for any unpaid Cost of the Work due him under Article 5, plus (1) the unpaid balance of the Fee computed upon the Cost of the Work to the date of termination at the rate of the percentage named in Article 6, or (2) if the Contractor's Fee be stated as a fixed sum, such an amount as will increase the payments on account of his Fee to a sum which bears the same ratio to the said fixed sum as the Cost of the Work at the time of termination bears to the adjusted Guaranteed Maximum Cost, if any, otherwise to a reasonable estimated Cost of the Work when completed. The Owner shall also pay to the Contractor fair compensation, either by purchase or rental at the election of the Owner, for any equipment retained. In case of such termination of the Contractor the Owner shall further assume and become liable for obligations, commitments and unsettled claims that the Contractor has previously undertaken or incurred in good faith in connection with said Work. The Contractor shall, as a condition of receiving the payments referred to in this Article 15, execute and deliver all such papers and take all such steps, including the legal assignment of his contractual rights, as the Owner may require for the purpose of fully vesting in himself the rights and benefits of the Contractor under such obligations or commitments.

ARTICLE 16

MISCELLANEOUS PROVISIONS

16.1 Terms used in this Agreement which are defined in the Contract Documents shall have the meanings designated in those Contract Documents.

16.2 The Contract Documents, which constitute the entire agreement between the Owner and the Contractor, are listed in Article 1 and, except for Modifications issued after execution of this Agreement, are enumerated as follows:

List below the Agreement, the Conditions of the Contract. (General, Supplementary, and other Conditions). The Drawings, the Specifications, and any Addenda and accepted alternates showing page or sheet numbers in all cases and dates where applicable.

This Standard Form Agreement Between Owner and Contractor, 1978 Edition of AIA Document AIII, General Conditions of the Contract for Construction, 1976 Edition of AIA Document A201 and modified thereon and attached hereto:

Summary of work consisting of nine (9) pages and attached hereto:

Sheet A-1, First Floor Plan, (MB), dated 06/07/yr-2, revised 07/11/yr-2, prepared by Architect

Sheet A-2, Second Floor Plan, (MB) " " " " "

Sheet A-3, Third Floor Plan, (MB) " " " " "

Sheet A-4, Fourth Floor Plan (MB " " " " "

Sheet A-5, First Floor Plan, (O) " " " " "

Sheet A-6, Second Floor Plan, (O) " " " " "

Sheet A-7, Third Floor Plan, (O) " " " " "

Sheet A-8, Fourth Floor Plan, (O) " " " " "

Sheet A-9, Floor Plan (Rec) " " " " "

This Agreement entered into as of the day and year first written above.

OWNER	CONTRACTOR
AREA CORPORATION	ROSS CONSTRUCTION, INC.
By: Michelle Greenwood	By: John Ross, Jr.
	September 15, YR-2

Summary of Work

A. <u>**LANDSCAPE**</u>:

1. Relocation of shrubbery, new landscaping, spreading of topsoil, seeding or sodding, bituminous paving and cobblestone paving will be accomplished by owner's landscape architect.

B. <u>**MASONRY**</u>:

1. Provide cement block units for foundation. Dash with a cement coating and float down where exposed.

2. Furnish and lay field veneer stone to match as closely as possible existing stone work and its pointing. This for the area shown on the drawings.

3. Build livingroom fireplace and bedroom fireplace with firebrick inner hearth and sidewalls.

4. Cast iron damper, flue liner where required to join existing. Outer hearth to be laid with available antique bricks. Facing to be plaster.

5. Dining room false fireplace to have Georgia Marble 1 thick polished for outer hearth and facing as shown on detail. Inner hearth to be brick laid dry.

6. Patch stone work where needed.

7. Patch stone work where present outside cellarway is altered.

8. New exterior doors to have blue stone sill.

C. <u>**MISCELLANEOUS IRON**</u>:

1. Furnish cast iron damper and angle lintel for livingroom fireplace.

2. Provide steel angles for stone veneer for exposed first floor and second floor windows.

D. <u>**LUMBER**</u>:

1. Sills or plates to be 20 x 60.

2. Exterior studs of house 20 x 60.

3. Sleepers for office, kitchen breakfast room to be 20 x 40 treated.

4. Floor joist for dressing room 20 x 100; ceiling joist 20 x 80.

5. Rafters for office 20 x 60.

6. Kitchen breakfast room ceiling joist to be 20 x 100. Rafters 20 x 80.

7. Cross bridging to be 10 x 30 Hemlock shingle lath.

8. Sub-flooring and roof sheathing to be 1/20 plywood.

9. Porch beams or joist to be 20 x 80 treated.

10. Miscellaneous blocking and furring as required.

11. 15-lb. slaters felt over exterior sheathing before siding which is to be exterior wood siding to match existing.

12. Porch floor to be tongue and groove, primed before laying.

E. MILLWORK:

1. Furnish new windows in size and type as shown on drawings.

2. Two case of six drawers with wood top shown in Dressing room.

3. Mantel breast units for Living room and Dining room as detailed. Antique mantel pieces furnished by owner to fit openings without renovations.

4. Cornice material as per detail.

5. Tongue and groove wood ceilings similar to existing.

6. Raised panel shutters as detailed and shown on drawings.

7. Interior ceiling molding for entire Living room, 1st floor hall and foyer.

8. Trim base and molding to be as shown on the Detail Drawing.

F. DAMPROOFING:

1. Since slabs are on grade, exterior foundations will be poured full and there will be no dampproofing as shown on foundation details.

2. Kitchen breakfast room extension wing will have polyethylene moisture sheet placed over the crushed stone before concrete is poured.

G. INSULATION:

1. New exterior walls of exposed rooms will have fiberglass batt insulation R19.

2. Ceilings of dressing room, kitchen breakfast room extension will have R35 fiberglass batts with foil face.

3. Semi-thick batts will be placed in the existing exterior walls that are furred out for the new kitchen.

4. Fill in dining room wall opening with batt insulation.

H. ROOFING: — Done by Owner.

I. METAL WORK: — Done by Owner except for Recreation Room:

1. Flashings and valleys to lead coated copper.

2. Gutters and downspouts to be of aluminum to match present down to grade only.

J. ROUGH HARDWARE:

1. Contractor to furnish nails, screws, caulking as required for the construction.

K. FINISH HARDWARE:

1. To be selected by the architect and owner from a cash allowance of Two Thousand, Five Hundred ($2,500.00) Dollars per unit.

L. <u>LATH & PLASTER</u>:

1. New walls, ceilings and openings to be patched to be lathed with 3/80 gypsum rock lath.

2. Ceiling of dressing room kitchen breakfast room to have chicken wire nailed to the lath as an additional reinforcing.

3. Plaster with scratch brown coat and finish with white hard wall plaster similar to the present.

4. Patching to be done in a good workmanlike manner.

5. There is no exterior stucco except inscription panel in the gable.

6. Face of living room fireplaces to be plastered.

M. <u>TILE & MARBLE</u>:

1. Master bathroom to have tile floor and walls patched out.

2. Furnish and place over a metal lath and mortar, new ceramic tile as selected in the tub recess full height.

3. Provide and install soap dish and two (2) ceramic towel bar units.

4. Furnish and install marble for dining room fireplace as shown on detail drawing with Georgia Marble – Solar Gray - 10 thick polished.

5. Install tile floor in powder room 105 with material supplied by owner.

6. Install tile backsplash in kitchen with materials supplied by owner allowing 30 sq. ft.

N. <u>WOOD FLOORS</u>:

1. Furnish and install 3/40 tongue and grooved oak plank flooring 40 - 60 - 80 widths screwed and plugged in kitchen, breakfast room.

2. Patch flooring where needed.

3. Sand, scrape and finish these new floors as well as the living room.

4. Furnish with one (1) coat of stain sealer, two (2) coats clear neutral sealer and one (1) coat of past wax.

5. Second floor: Furnish and install 3/40 x 2-1/40 tongue and groove select red oak strip in dressing room area. Sand and finish as above. Also clean and wax floor in Master bedroom when work is completed.

O. <u>PAINTING</u>:

1. Prime coat all four sides before erection of millwork.

2. Existing door frames where new doors are installed are to be touched up and one (1) coat of matching paint color.

3. Interior millwork to be back primed also and given a coat of undercoater and a final coat of semi-gloss enamel.

4. New plaster walls and ceilings to receive three (3) coats color as selected.

5. Existing plaster would receive two (2) coats of paint.

6. Interior fireplace brick is to be painted.

P. BATHROOM ACCESSORIES:

1. New shower doors in master bathrooms.

2. New accessories.

3. New additional accessories included under tile work.

Q. STORM SASH:

1. Furnish and install white enamel finish aluminum combination storm sash and screens on the new double hung window frames of the house renovations and additions.

R. H.V.A.C.: — Plans to be approved.

S. PLUMBING:

1. Disconnect and remove present kitchen plumbing items and cap lines as required.

2. Disconnect and remove tub from second floor bathrooms.

3. Furnish and install new white Jacuzzi (Nova) 500 x 420 x 180 deep bathtub complete with whirlpool, faucet, less shower and new drain; replace existing toilets & install new according to drawings.

4. Furnish and install two (2) outside hose faucets per unit.

5. Furnish and install water and waste line plumbing for new kitchen units including connecting a double-bowl sink, garbage disposal, dishwasher, and ice maker. These furnished under kitchen equipment.

6. It is assumed the present septic system is large enough in capacity to handle the additional plumbing work.

T. ELECTRICAL:

1. Replace existing electrical service with new 400 AMP service with new panel in basements.

2. Disconnect or relocate outlets and switches in alteration locations.

3. Allow the following number of connections per unit:

Item	
Receptacles	30
Outlets	36
Switches	27
Power or equip. connec.	13

4. Owner to purchase and deliver assembled fixtures with necessary lamps except porcelain sockets and two double flood light units.

5. Electrician to hang fixtures and furnish electrical underwriters' certificate for completed electrical work.

6. No smoke, fire or alarm work is included for this project.

U. GENERAL:

1. Owner will obtain local building permit from the City.

2. General Contractor to coordinate their work with owner's landscape architect and any other trades.

3. Contractor to clean and haul away building debris and leave the premises broom clean.

4. Temporary water, electric, or heat will be furnished by the owner. Contractor to use care in their use.

5. Architect to cooperate with all parties for selections, approvals and coordination of work. He is to be the interpreter of the intent of various trade work.

KITCHEN EQUIPMENT:

1. Thermodor CMT-21

   Combination Micro/Convention Ovens — Self Cleaning

   Black glass doors

2. Thermodor "Tradewind"

   Ventilator ducted

   (Install in wood hood)

3. Subzero Model #3211 / 48 wide side-by-side Refrigerator

4. Kitchen Aid KDS-21 Dishwasher — Superba

5. Kitchen Aid KWS-200 Garbage Disposal — Superba

6. Thermodor TMH 34-SS Stainless Steel — 4-burner cooktop

7. Kitchen Aid KCS-200 Trash Compactor

8. Elkay DLR-3322-10 Stainless Steel Sink - Double bowl

KITCHEN CABINETS:

1. Cabinetry as manufactured by Pioneer Craftsman.

2. Wood specie to be Oak — Door style Wm. Penn.

3. Satin finish / Natural interior.

4. Hardware from standard selection board.

COUNTERTOPS:

1. Corian — 3/4O thick top with additional 3/4O at edge with ogee routed detail.

2. 3/4O thick x 1-1/2O high backsplash at countertop to receive tile.

FINANCIAL INFORMATION ON ROSS CONSTRUCTION CO., INC.

Ross Constr. Co. Inc.	Unequal	Unequal	Unequal	Unequal
Mitchell Wiggins & Co.	Dec 31	Dec 31	Dec 31	Dec 31
Rme (000s)	YR-6	YR-5	YR-4	YR-3
INCOME STATEMENT	12	12	12	12
Net Sales	41916	39863	45553	63096
Cost of Goods Sold	32818	31762	33660	47947
GROSS PROFIT/REVENUES	9098	8101	11893	15149
0000				
Sales, Gen. & Admin. Expense	4354	4476	4466	5111
Depreciation	1558	1508	1414	1562
				000
OPERATING PROFIT	3186	2117	6013	6013
Interest/Short-Term Debt				
Interest/Existing Long-Term Debt				
Interest/New Long-Term Debt				
Total Interest Expense	806	728	256	113
Interest Income	199	89	110	55
Other Income	433	341	666	616
Other Expense	651	1065	877	1034
Total Other	−825	−1363	−357	−476
NET INCOME BEFORE TAX	2361	754	5656	8000
Income Taxes	1361	291	2622	3699
NET INCOME BEFORE EXTR. ITEMS	1012	463	3034	4301
Extraordinary Items	17	11	244	23
NET INCOME	1029	474	3278	4324
Preferred Dividends	0	0	0	0
Common Dividends Distributed	478	475	592	794
Retained Earnings Prior Period	0	14771	14771	17455
Adjmts. to Retained Earnings	14771	0	0	0

RETAINED EARNINGS	14771	14771	14455	20986
Net Sales Growth	%	−4.90°	14.27	38.51
Gross Margin	%21.71	20.32	26.11	24.01
SG&A Expense/Net Sales	%10.39	11.23	9.80	8.10
Operating Profit Margin	%7.60	5.31	13.20	13.43
NPBT Margin	%5.63	1.89	12.41	12.68
NPAT Margin	%2.45	1.19	7.19	6.85
ASSETS				
Cash & Equivalent	1379	999	2997	878
Marketable Securities	0	0	0	0
Accounts Receivable—Net	3056	3642	5746	7076
Inventory	8467	6276	6351	8570
Other Current Assets	245	342	79	67
CURRENT ASSETS	13147	11259	15173	16591
Gross Fixed Assets	26174	26854	27557	31330
Less Accumulated Depreciation	17571	19508	21208	22838
Fixed Assets—Net	8603	7346	6349	8492
Prepaid & Deferred Expenses	50	56	42	44
Long-Term Investments	58	70	45	1858
Other Noncurrent Assets	595	425	558	858
Intangibles	67	58	50	76
NONCURRENT ASSETS	9373	7955	7044	11328
TOTAL ASSETS	22520	19215	22217	27918
LIABILITIES				
Current Maturities				
Exist L T D	865	865	615	82
Current Maturities New L T Debt				
Notes Payable	0	1000	0	0
Additional Short-Term Debt				
DEBT IN CURRENT LIABILITIES	865	1865	615	82
Accounts Payable	1562	1262	2285	3147
Income Tax Payable	1309	0	975	420
Miscellaneous Accruals	1517	1381	1585	1965
Other Current Liabilities	0	0	0	0
CURRENT LIABILITIES	5253	4508	5460	5614
Existing Long-Term Debt	2084	1218	602	2520
New Long-Term Debt	0	0	0	0
Other Noncurrent Liabilities	173	183	193	202

Deferred Taxes	0	0	0	0
TOTAL SENIOR DEBT	7510	5909	6255	8336
Subordinated Debt	0	0	0	0
TOTAL LIABILITIES	7510	5909	6255	8336
NET WORTH				
Reserves	0	0	0	0
Preferred Stock	0	0	0	0
Common Stock	754	754	754	754
Capital Surplus, Other Equity	1031	1025	1025	1038
Less: Treasury Stock	−1544	−3243	−3273	−3196
Retained Earnings	14771	14771	17455	20986
TOTAL NET WORTH	15012	13307	15961	19582
TOTAL LIABILITIES & NET WORTH	22522	19216	22216	27917
Receivables in Days	27	33	46	41
Inventory in Days	94	72	69	65
Payables in Days	17	15	25	24
Current Ratio	2.50	2.50	2.78	2.96
Quick Ratio	0.84	1.03	1.60	1.42
Working Capital	7894	6752	9712	10977
Total Debt/Net Worth	0.50	0.44	0.39	0.43
Total Debt/Tangible Net Worth	0.53	0.47	0.41	0.45
CASHFLOW				
Sales—Net	39863	45553	63096	
Changes in Receivables	−586	−2104	−1331	
Cash from Sales	39277	43449	61765	
Cost of Goods Sold	−31762	−33660	−47947	
Change in Inventories	2191	−74	−2220	
Change in Payables	−300	1023	862	
Cash Production Costs	−29871	−32711	−49305	
Gross Cash Margins	9406	10738	12460	
SG&A Expense	−4476	−4466	−5111	
Change in Prepaids	−6	13	−1	
Change in Accruals	−136	205	380	
Cash Operation Expense	−4618	−4248	−4732	
Cash after Operations	−4787	6490	7728	
Miscellaneous Cash Income	−268	10	−616	
Income Taxes Paid	−1872	−1375	−4256	

Net Cash after Operations	2647	5125	2856
Interest Expense	−728	−256	−113
Dividends Paid	−475	−592	−794
Financing Costs	−1203	−848	−907
Net Cash Income	1444	4277	1494
Current Portion Long-Term Debt	−865	−865	−615
Cash after Debt Amortization	579	3412	1334
Capital Expenditures	−242	−409	−3730
Long-Term Investments	−12	26	−1813
Financing Surplus/(Requirements)	325	3029	−4209
Change in Short-Term Debt	1000	−1000	0
Change in Long-Term Debt	−1	−1	1999
Change in Equity	−1705	−30	90
Total External Financing	−706	−1031	−2089
Cash after Financing	−380	1998	−2119
ACTUAL CHANGE IN CASH	−380	1998	−2119
Traditional Cash Flow	1983	4690	5887

Defendants' Exhibit 3

From: JackAnders1@zeronet.nita

To: DougLi@LiBuilders.nita

Date sent: 7/9/YR-2

Subject: Cost overruns

Copies to:

Priority:

Hey, I'm pretty angry about those cost overruns from the electrician. It's urgent I see you about this. Call me as soon as possible. Jack

Defendants' Exhibit 4

Defendants' Exhibit 5

Ross Construction @ Warsaw Project - 11 Jul
Score one for Ross Construction: Jr 1, Chink 0.

Jury Instructions

Jury Instructions[1]
Part I. Preliminary Instructions

Introduction

You have been selected as jurors and have taken an oath to try this case well and truly. This trial will last one day.

During the progress of the trial there will be periods of time when the court recesses. During those periods of time, you must not talk about this case among yourselves or with anyone else.

During the trial, do not talk to any of the parties, their lawyers, or any of the witnesses.

If any attempt is made by anyone to talk to you concerning the matters under consideration, you should report the fact to the court immediately.

You should keep an open mind. You should not form or express an opinion during the trial and should reach no conclusion in this case until you have heard all of the evidence, the arguments of counsel, and the final instructions as to the law, which will be given to you by the Court.

Conduct of the Trial

First, the attorneys will have an opportunity to make opening statements. These statements are not evidence and should be considered only as a preview of what the attorneys expect the evidence will be.

Following the opening statements, witnesses will be called to testify. They will be placed under oath and questioned by the attorneys. Documents and other tangible exhibits may be received as evidence. If an exhibit is given to you to examine, you should examine it carefully, individually, and without comment.

Counsel have the right to object when testimony or other evidence that he or she believes is not admissible is offered.

When the Court sustains an objection to a question, the jurors must disregard the question and the answer if one has been given and draw no inference from the question or the answer or speculate as to what the witness would have said if permitted to answer. Evidence stricken from the record must likewise be disregarded.

When the Court sustains an objection to any evidence, the jurors must disregard such evidence.

When the Court overrules an objection to any evidence, the jurors must not give such evidence any more weight than if the objection had not been made.

When the evidence is completed, the attorneys will make final statements. These final statements are not evidence, but are given to assist you in evaluating the evidence. The attorneys also are permitted to

---

1. These instructions are borrowed or adapted from a number of sources, including Federal Pattern Jury Instructions and Pattern Jury Instructions from California, Colorado, Florida, Illinois, Indiana, North Carolina, and Washington, and from the NITA case file, *Doyle v. Nita Power & Light C.*

argue to attempt to persuade you to reach a particular verdict. You may accept or reject those arguments as you see fit.

Just before you retire to consider your verdict, I will give you further instructions on the law that applies to this case.

PART II. FINAL INSTRUCTIONS

Introduction

Members of the jury, the evidence and arguments in this case have been completed, and I now will instruct you as to the law. These instructions state the law applicable to this case, and it is your duty to follow all of these instructions. You must not single out certain instructions and disregard others.

It is your duty to determine the facts and to determine them only from the evidence in this case. You are to apply the law to the facts and in this way decide the case. You must not be governed or influenced by sympathy or prejudice for or against any party in this case. Your verdict must be based on evidence and not on speculation, guess, or conjecture.

From time to time, it has been the duty of the Court to rule on the admissibility of evidence. You must not concern yourselves with the reasons for these rulings. You should disregard questions and exhibits that were withdrawn or to which objections were sustained. You also should disregard testimony and exhibits that the Court has refused or stricken.

The evidence that you should consider consists only of testimony of the witnesses and the exhibits that the Court has received.

Any evidence that was received for a limited purpose should not be considered by you for any other purpose. You should consider all the evidence in light of your own observations and experiences in life.

Neither by these instructions nor by any ruling or remark that I have made do I mean to indicate any opinion as to the facts or as to what your verdict should be.

Credibility of Witnesses

You are the sole judges of the credibility of the witnesses and of the weight to be given the testimony of each. In determining what credit is to be given to any witness, you may take into account his or her ability and opportunity to observe; his or her manner and appearance while testifying; any interest, bias, or prejudice he or she may have; the reasonableness of his or her testimony considered in the light of all the evidence; and any other factors that bear on the believability and weight of the witness's testimony.

Expert Witnesses

You have heard evidence in this case from witnesses who have testified as experts. The law allows experts to express opinions on subjects involving their special knowledge, training, skill, experience, or research; but while their opinions are allowed to be given, it is entirely within the province of the jury to determine what weight shall be given their testimony. Jurors are not bound by the testimony of experts; their testimony is to be weighed as that of any other witness.

Employee of a Party

The fact that a witness was (or is) employed by one of the defendants and the testimony you have heard of the witness's relations with the employer may be considered by you in determining whether his or her testimony in any way was influenced by his or her employment relationship with the defendant.

Direct and Circumstantial Evidence

The law recognizes two kinds of evidence: direct and circumstantial. Direct evidence proves a fact directly. Circumstantial evidence proves a fact indirectly in that it follows from other facts or circumstances according to common experience and observations in life. An eyewitness provides a common example of direct evidence, while human footprints are circumstantial evidence that a person was present.

The law makes no distinction between direct and circumstantial evidence as to the degree or amount of proof required, and each should be considered according to whatever weight or value it may have. You should consider and evaluate all of the evidence in arriving at your verdict.

Corporate Party

One of the parties in this case is a corporation. It is entitled to the same fair treatment as an individual would receive under like circumstances. You should decide the case with the same impartiality you would use in deciding a case involving only individuals.

Since a corporation can act only through its officers, or employees, or other agents, any negligent act or omission of an officer, or employee, or other agent of a corporation, in the performance of his duties, is held in law to be the negligence of the corporation.

Burden of Proof

When I say that a party has the burden of proof on an issue, or use the expressions "if you find," "if you decide," or "by a preponderance of the evidence," I mean that you must be persuaded from a consideration of all the evidence in the case that the issue on which a party has the burden of proof is more probably true than not true.

Any findings of fact you make must be based on probabilities, not possibilities. They may not be based on surmise, speculation, or conjecture.

Theories and Defense

The plaintiff and the defendants have various theories and defenses in this case. I will now instruct you as to each theory and its corresponding defense(s).

The plaintiff brings two causes of action against the defendant. If you find that the plaintiff has shown by a preponderance of evidence that either cause of action exists, then you must find for the plaintiff. The plaintiff's burdens are as follows:

1. Tortious Interference with Contract Rights (Plaintiff's Burden)

A. The elements required for a showing of a tortious interference with contract rights are:

1. The existence of a valid contractual relationship;

2. Knowledge of the contractual relationship on the part of the interferer;

3. Intentional improper acts amounting to interference inducing or causing a breach or termination of the contractual relationship; and

4. Resultant damage to the party whose contractual relationship has been disrupted.

B. Definition of Contract

A contract is an agreement between two parties. There must be an offer by one party and an acceptance by the other party for mutual consideration. An offer is a proposal of the terms on which a person will enter into an agreement if the offer is accepted by the person to whom it is made. An acceptance is an unconditional promise to be bound by the terms of the offer.

In determining whether there is a contract, you should look to the intent of the parties to the contract as outwardly or objectively demonstrated to each other by their words and deeds.

There is no legal requirement that parties agree on all matters incidental to their agreement before they can intend to be bound. Thus, even if certain matters were left for future negotiations, those matters may not have been regarded as essential to the agreement between the parties.

C. Definition of Knowledge

In order for you to find for the plaintiff, you must determine that the defendant knew of the existence of this contract. For this purpose, it is not necessary that defendant had actual knowledge of this specific contract. It is sufficient that defendant had knowledge of facts which, if followed by inquiry ordinarily made by a reasonable and prudent person, would have led to a disclosure of the contractual relationship between plaintiff and Ms. Greenwood. This is sometimes referred to as "constructive knowledge."

D. Definition of Mailbox Rule

The mailbox rule is in effect: if you find that a person accepted an offer, then there is a contract. Acceptance can be revoked if revoked before the acceptance was delivered. An acceptance is deemed delivered in Nita at the time it is put in the mail.

2. Tortious Interference with Prospective Economic Advantage

A. The elements required for a showing of a cause of action for tortious interference with prospective economic advantage are:

1. the existence of a business relationship or expectancy with a probability of future economic benefit to plaintiff;

2. defendants' knowledge of the relationship or expectancy;

3. malice on the part of the defendant inducing or causing a termination of the relationship or expectancy;

4. resultant damage to the party whose relationship has been disrupted.

B. Definition of Malice

A false statement is made maliciously if the person making it knows that the statement is false. A false statement is made maliciously even though the person making it did not know that it was false if 1) it is made with intent to interfere with another person's interests or a deliberate desire to do another person harm, or 2) it is made recklessly, without regard to the consequences, and under circumstances from which defendant as a reasonably prudent person should have anticipated that injury to another would follow.

If you find that the statement was not made maliciously, your verdict will be for the defendant.

Where there is evidence that the defendants' primary and overriding purpose is to injure his victim in his reputation, trade, business or profession, motivated by hatred, spite, or ill-will, the element of malice is established. This is true regardless of any additional motives entertained by the defendant to benefit himself or persons other than the victim.

C. Definition of Proximate Cause

The plaintiff must prove by a preponderance of the evidence that the conduct of defendant proximately caused the breach of the contract that resulted in his injury. A result is proximately caused by an act or omission whenever it appears that the act or omission played a substantial part in actually bringing about or causing such result. This is sometimes referred to as the "but for" test: should you find that but for the conduct of defendant, the breach of plaintiff's contract would not have occurred, then defendant proximately caused the breach.

3. Defamation/Slander

The plaintiff, Doug Li, claims that the defendant, John Ross, defamed him in four specific instances (*see* Complaint).

The plaintiff claims that the defendant's statements injured his reputation by subjecting him to contempt, ridicule, humiliation, and scorn in the community, and precluded him from obtaining and/or continuing a business relationship.

The defendant denies that he defamed the plaintiff or that his actions precluded the plaintiff from obtaining a business relationship. The defendant further claims that his statements were opinions, were privileged, and that they were true.

The plaintiff claims that the defendant defamed him in four different instances. The plaintiff has the burden of proving his claim of defamation. If he proves that he was defamed in any one of the four instances, then he has satisfied his burden of proof. He may prove all or any one of the four instances of defamation, but he must meet his burden of proof for at least one.

A. The elements required for a showing of a cause of action for defamation/slander are:

1. that the defendant made the alleged statement;

2. that the statement was defamatory;

3. that the defendant published the defamatory statement to someone other than the plaintiff;

4. that the plaintiff was injured; and

5. that the plaintiff's injuries were caused by the defendant's defamatory statement.

B. Definition of Defamatory

A statement is defamatory if it tends to harm the plaintiff's reputation and thereby lower him in the opinion of others or discourage others from associating or dealing with him.

In determining whether a statement was defamatory, you should consider the plain and natural meaning of the words, construed in the plain and popular sense in which people understand them.

In determining whether the statement defamed the plaintiff, you should consider the statement as a whole and not dwell on isolated words within the statement.

[Note: *Opinion*. A statement is not defamatory if it is mere opinion. It is for the Court, and not the jury, to determine as a matter of law whether alleged defamatory words constitute mere opinion or are statements of fact. *See Chaves v. Johnson*.]

C. Definition of Defamatory Per Se

A statement that impugns another in his trade or business is defamatory per se; that is, it is by its very nature defamatory. Furthermore, it is presumed that a person so defamed has been injured.

If you find from the evidence that the defendant impugned the plaintiff in his trade or business, then the defendant's statement is defamatory per se and your verdict must be for the plaintiff, unless you find that the defendant has established a defense of truth or privilege.

C. Definition of Publication

The term "publication" or "published" means the intentional or negligent communication of a defamatory statement, either written or oral, to a person other than the plaintiff.

D. Truth Is a Defense

If you find that the defendant made the alleged statement or words substantially similar, that it defamed the plaintiff, and that it was published to someone other than the plaintiff, then you must consider whether the statement was substantially true. Substantial truth is an absolute defense.

Substantial truth does not require that every word be true. Substantial truth means that the substance or gist of a statement is true.

The burden is on the defendant to prove that the statement was substantially true. If the defendant proves the truth of the statement, then it is an absolute defense, and your verdict shall be for the defendant on that statement.

[Note: If the Court determines that the plaintiff is a public figure, or the speech is a matter of public concern, then the burden of proof will shift to the plaintiff to show that the statements made were false.]

E. Definition of Qualified Privilege

A defamatory statement that is published to another is protected by a qualified privilege if it was made on any subject in which the party making the communication has an important interest or duty—either legal, moral, business, or social—if such communication was made to another person having a corresponding interest or duty. Thus, a defamatory statement is protected by a qualified privilege if *both* parties to the communication have either an important interest or duty with regard to the statement. The statement must, of course, be made for the purpose and within the scope of that common interest or duty.

Negative character references, or even references which are less than enthusiastic, are by their very nature defamatory. There are, however, very obvious legal, moral, business, and social interests in having honest and forthright character references. Therefore, a defamatory statement that is made in the context of a character reference is protected by a qualified privilege.

[Note: The Court may rule, as a matter of law, that the statements allegedly made by the defendant in this case are protected by a qualified privilege. If the Court so rules, then the defendant must be given the benefit of that privilege. The privilege, however, is not an absolute defense to a defamatory statement, and the following instructions would be given to the jury. Note also: The instructions below, requiring a finding of malice, would also be given if the Court determines that the plaintiff was a public figure or the speech was a matter of public concern.]

F. A Qualified Privilege Is a Qualified Defense

The privilege is qualified because it does not protect a defamatory statement that is made with malice or with a reckless disregard for the interests of another person.

Thus, even though the defendant's statements are protected by a qualified privilege, it is not an absolute defense. The plaintiff may recover if he proves the statements were made with malice toward him or with a reckless disregard for his interests.

E. Definition of Malice

A person acts with "malice" if:

1. he makes a false statement concerning another, with knowledge of its falsity; *or*

2. he makes a false statement concerning another without knowledge of its falsity, but for the specific purpose of injuring that person.

F. Definition of Reckless Disregard

A person acts with "reckless disregard for the interests of another person" if he recklessly makes a false statement concerning the person.

A person acts "recklessly" when he consciously disregards and is indifferent to:

1. the truth or falsity of the statement, *and*

2. the probable consequences of the statement, and such disregard and indifference is a gross departure from the care that a reasonable person would exercise in the situation. Recklessness is an indifference to the rights of others and to whether wrong or injury is done to them.

It is not necessary to prove that the defendant deliberately intended to injure the plaintiff. It is sufficient if the defendant, indifferent to the consequence, acted with a reckless disregard for the truth or falsity of the statement and in such a way that the natural and probable consequence of his act was injury to the plaintiff.

G. Factors in Determining Malice or Reckless Disregard

In determining whether the defendant acted with malice or with a reckless disregard for the plaintiff's interests, you may consider the following factors:

1. Did the defendant reasonably rely on the circumstances known to him when he made the defamatory statement?

2. Did the defendant make the statement in good faith and believing it to be true?

3. Did the defendant act maliciously or recklessly in making the statement?

4. Did the defendant act with spite or ill will toward the plaintiff; that is, did the defendant intend to injure the plaintiff's reputation, good name, or feelings;

5. Did the defendant attempt to minimize any harm to the plaintiff by apologizing or retracting a defamatory statement with reasonable promptness and fairness after determining the statement was false?

If you find that the defendant acted with malice or with a reckless disregard for the interests of the plaintiff, then the qualified privilege has been abused and is not applicable, and you must find for the plaintiff. The burden of proof is on the plaintiff to establish that the defendant acted with malice or a reckless disregard for her interests.

Compensatory Damages

If you find that the plaintiff is entitled to relief by a greater weight of the evidence, you must award damages necessary to compensate the plaintiff for his loss. The damages recoverable are those proximately caused by the defendant's actions, including those that would return the plaintiff to the position he would have been in had the defendant not acted and any future damages resulting therefrom.

[Note: *Re Defamation Damages*. If the Court finds that the plaintiff is a public figure or that the speech is a matter of public concern, then the Court will require that the plaintiff show *actual injury by clear and convincing evidence*.]

Future Damages

Future damages may be recovered by the plaintiff if the damages were reasonably certain to occur or follow. The fact that the measure of damages is uncertain should not preclude the award of future damages as long as the cause of the damages is certain by a preponderance of the evidence. Thus, mere speculation should not preclude the award of future damages.

Punitive Damages

If you find that the plaintiff is entitled to be compensated for his damages, and if you further believe by the greater weight of the evidence that the defendant acted with malice toward the plaintiff or acted under circumstances amounting to a willful and wanton disregard of the plaintiff's rights, then you may also award punitive damages to the plaintiff to punish the defendant for his actions and to serve as an example to prevent others from acting in a similar way. If you award punitive damages, you may take into consideration the wealth of the defendant in determining the amount of punitive damages to be awarded.

If you award punitive damages, you must state separately in your verdict the amount you allow as compensatory damages and the amount you allow as punitive damages.

Definition of Malice for Punitive Damages

Malice, for awarding punitive damages, is a sinister or corrupt motive such as hatred, personal spite, ill will, or a desire to injure the plaintiff.

GENERAL VERDICT FORM

IN THE CIRCUIT COURT OF NITA CITY, NITA

Doug Li, dba Li Builders)	
)	
Plaintiff)	
)	
v.)	**VERDICT**
)	
John Ross and)	
Ross Construction Co., Inc.)	No. C-1234
)	
Defendants)	

WE THE JURY AND EACH OF FIND:

(Circle one and fill in the appropriate amount)

Compensatory Damages

For the plaintiff Doug Li in the amount of $_____ against the defendants John Ross and Ross Construction Co. Inc.

For the Defendants.

Punitive Damages

For the plaintiff Doug Li in the amount of $_____ against the defendants John Ross and Ross Construction Co. Inc.

For the Defendants.

_____
Foreperson

CPSIA information can be obtained
at www.ICGtesting.com
Printed in the USA
BVHW012328041219
565694BV00009B/69/P

9 781601 564320